Walking Ad

Walking Adventures on Anglesey

Dafydd Meirion

© Text: Dafydd Meirion 2004

© Pictures: Dylan Williams

Copyright © by Gwasg Carreg Gwalch 2004.
All rights reserved. No part of this publication
may be reproduced or transmitted, in any form
or by any means, without permission.

ISBN: 0-86381-944-3

Cover Design: Sian Parri

Published by
Gwasg Carreg Gwalch,
12 Iard yr Orsaf, Llanrwst, Wales, LL26 0EH.
01492 642031   01492 641502
Printed and published in Wales.

Contents

Walking Adventures on Anglesey 8

Notes for adults 10

1. The Battle of the Bridge of Boats (Brynsiencyn) 13

2. Saint Dwynwen – Patron Saint of Welsh Lovers
   (Llanddwyn) 21

3. The Wreckers of Crigyll (Rhosneigr) 29

4. Madam Wen – The Welsh Highwaywoman (Caergeiliog) .35

5. Tyger the Brave Dog (Rhoscolyn) 43

6. The Thief of Dyfrydog and the girl amongst the Fairies
   (Llandyfrydog) 49

7. The Bonesetters of Anglesey (Cemaes) 57

8. The sinking of the Royal Charter (Moelfre) 63

9. The Witches of Llanddona (Llanddona) 71

10. The Snake of Penhesgyn
    (Penmynydd) 77

ANGLESEY

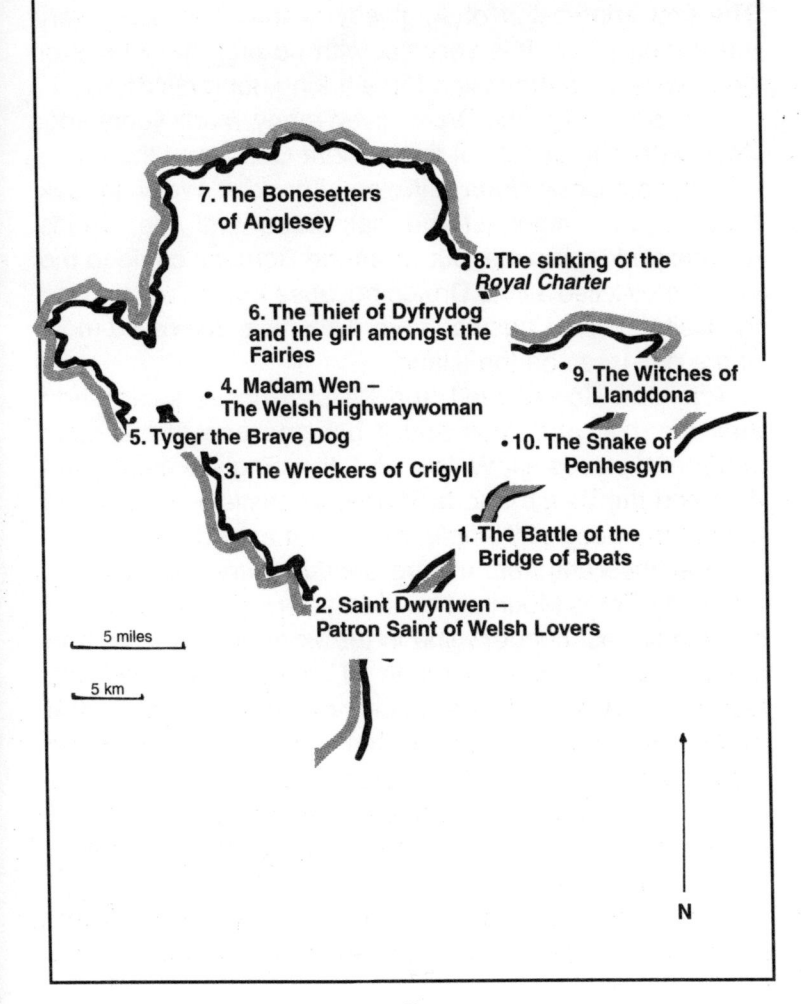

7. The Bonesetters of Anglesey
8. The sinking of the *Royal Charter*
6. The Thief of Dyfrydog and the girl amongst the Fairies
4. Madam Wen – The Welsh Highwaywoman
5. Tyger the Brave Dog
9. The Witches of Llanddona
3. The Wreckers of Crigyll
10. The Snake of Penhesgyn
1. The Battle of the Bridge of Boats
2. Saint Dwynwen – Patron Saint of Welsh Lovers

5 miles

5 km

N

Walking Adventures on Anglesey

The first impression of Anglesey is that it is not a very interesting place. It is very flat with no high mountains or deep valleys, but the island has a long, long history.

It was here that the Druids lived many, many years ago. They were the priests of the ancient Celts, and the name comes from Derwyddon in Welsh after derw, Welsh for oak trees. It was amongst the oak trees that the Druids worshipped their gods. But when the Romans came to the island they killed all the Druids because it was they that led the Celts to battle against them. They also destroyed most of the oak trees on the island.

After the Romans left, the Welsh Princes established their court at Aberffraw and it became one of the most important places in Wales. But the English came and defeated the Welsh and built a huge castle in Beaumaris to stop the people of Anglesey from attacking them.

Over the centuries, mining became very important on Anglesey. Parys Mountain on the eastern side of the island had the largest copper mine in the world at one time, and the port of Amlwch was one of the busiest in Wales. Because Anglesey is an island, many ships sailed the waters around its shores and many lives were lost when these ships went on the rocks. Anglesey was a very remote place until the bridges over the Menai Strait and the A5 across the island were built, but now there are roads going in every direction.

Here is an opportunity for you to hear some of the stories from Anglesey over the centuries – the people, the battles, the shipwrecks and the various animals and monsters. You can read the story and then go for a walk to see where these stories happened. And while you are walking you can answer the questions at the end of each story.

There is space also at the end of the book to make a list of all the birds, animals and plants that you have seen on your walks. Once you have all the answers, send a copy of these pages to the publishers to receive your certificate.

This is to confirm that

....

answered all the questions in

Walking Adventures on Anglesey

Gwasg Carreg Gwalch

Notes for adults

All of these routes are circular ones, starting and finishing in the same place. They are between an hour and a half and three and a half hours long. At the beginning of each route, there is either parking space or a bus stop (apart from Nos 2 and 7). Most of the routes take you along paths or beaches, but sometimes it is necessary to walk along a road with a pavement. On very rare occasions you will have to walk along a country road with no pavement. You are advised to walk in a single file facing the traffic.

Some of these routes follow the official Anglesey Coastal Path above the shore. Nevertheless, you should keep an eye on the children on these paths and make sure that they do not go too near the edge.

You should wear suitable shoes, and remember to wear warm clothing in winter. Also take with you waterproof clothing – even in summer! It would be a sensible idea to look at the weather forecast before you start.

Shops and cafes, when available, are noted on the routes, but it would be a good idea to take some food and something to drink with you.

If you are taking your dog with you, keep it on a lead – and remember to clean after it. You should keep to the paths at all times, and don't wander on to agricultural land.

The length of the walk and the time needed is noted at the beginning of each route. This is only an estimate of the time needed; I'm sure that you will want to have a rest every so often to look at the magnificent views, to have a picnic or to examine some of the wonders of Anglesey. You should, therefore, allow plenty of time for each walk.

Maps: The maps in the book give only a rough idea of the route, although the instructions are detailed enough for you to follow. If you want detailed maps of the island, you should buy the OS Explorer 262 (west) and Explorer 263 (east).

Enjoy your walks!

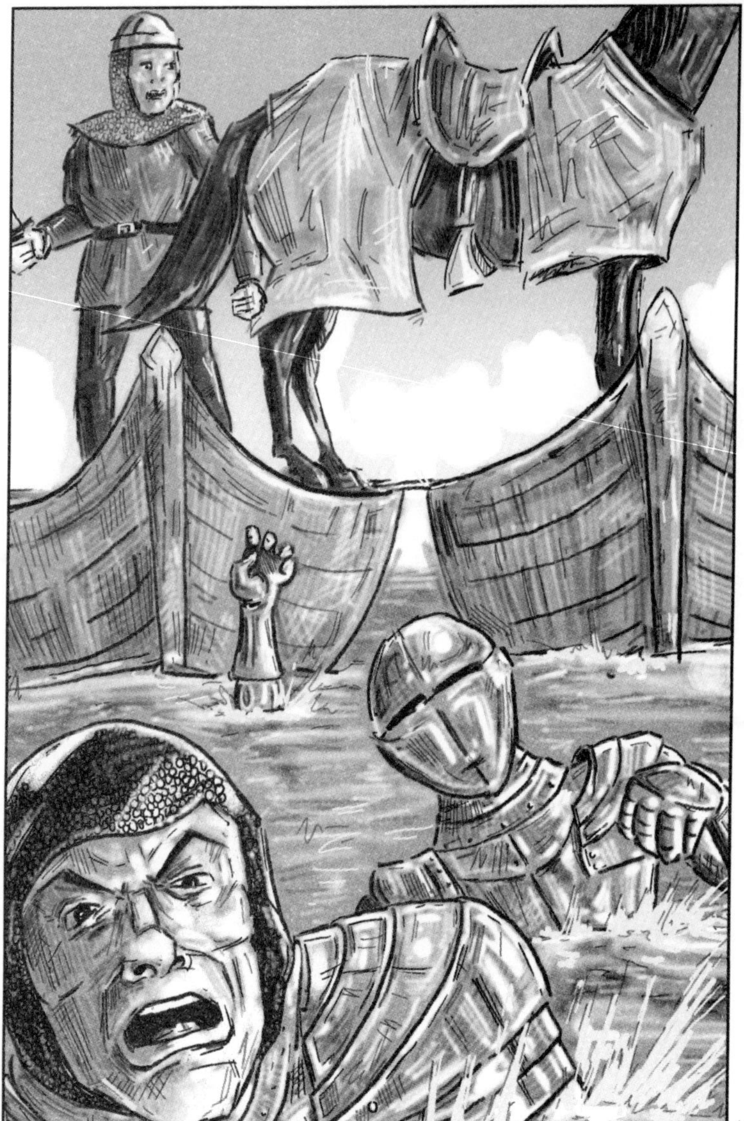

The Battle of the Bridge of Boats

THE STORY

Anglesey, with its large farms and productive fields, is a very fertile area. In the olden days, the island supplied most of the wheat and oats for people and animals living on the mainland. Because of this, when the English forces attacked the princes of Gwynedd in the 12th and 13th centuries, it was very important for them to capture the island.

Llywelyn ap Gruffudd had been crowned Prince of Wales and had been ruling the country for many years. But the English were not happy with this situation and in 1282 King Edward I decided to attack the Welsh.

Anglesey is not a very good place to defend. There are plenty of beaches for enemy forces to land here, and there are no mountains for the inhabitants to hide in. And for these reasons, it did not take long for Edward's forces to capture the island.

The next step was to attack the mainland. The English had already stopped food supplies from getting there, and now they were preparing a large force to attack the Welsh across the water. But it was not only English soldiers that were in Edward's army. There were also many knights from France and Spain, under the command of Luc de Tany from Gascony – all mercenaries paid to attack the

Welsh.

Of course, at that time, there were no bridges crossing the Menai Strait. Boats or ferries were used to carry people, animals and foodstuffs across the water. Edward's forces had brought hundreds of boats with them from Chester, but they did not use them to row the soldiers over to the mainland. This would have taken them too much time. They placed the boats in one long line across the Menai Strait and then placed planks of wood across them to form a long bridge.

The Welsh, in their hiding places in the mountains on the opposite side, could see this work going on. Because the Welsh forces were much smaller than the English forces, there was no point in them attacking. They therefore stayed hidden amongst the trees and bushes waiting for their chance.

One by one, Edward's soldiers began crossing the bridge of boats. The knights in their heavy suits of armour went first with the foot soldiers following. They formed one long line across the bridge, all glad that there was no sign of the Welsh soldiers.

The first knights reached the mainland and began cantering up the hillside. Suddenly, the Welsh jumped out of the trees shouting loudly. The horses were frightened and the knights fell off them to be killed by the Welsh.

The knights still crossing the bridge of boats could see what was happening, and they did not want to be killed by the Welsh. So they tried to turn back, but since there were so many of them in one long line, this was not possible. The knights at the front were pushing trying to get back, and the boats started to sway.

Suddenly, one of the boats capsized, then another one. And then the knights started to fall into the water. As they were wearing their heavy suits of armour, they couldn't swim to the shore and many of them drowned. Then the tide turned and the bridge of boats started to come apart. All the knight and soldiers fell into the sea. Between those that drowned or were killed by the Welsh, Edward lost 13 knights (including their leader Luc de Tany), 17 gentry and about 200 soldiers.

This battle was a great victory for Llywelyn and the Welsh forces. The battle is called the Battle of the Bridge of Boats or the Battle of Moel y Don although no one is certain where exactly the fighting took place. At one time, there was a slate plaque on the mainland in Y Felinheli, across the water to Moel y Don, commemorating the victory. But many historians say that it took place further to the east.

But wherever it took place, the Welsh were victorious against superior English forces on that day.

THE WALK

From Moel y Don along the shores of the Menai Strait to Tal y Foel, where the Sea Zoo, Foel Farm and the Chocolate Shop is located, and back along wooded paths. 12 miles – 3 ½ hours

This journey is longer than the rest, but worth the effort as it takes you along the shores of the Menai Strait with its magnificent views, and returning along paths that take you through fields and forests. About half way, you can rest at either the Sea Zoo or Foel Farm.

You should do this journey when the tide is out, because when the tide is in there are two places where you can't go past as the water reaches private land. Also,

The Battle of the Bridge of Boats

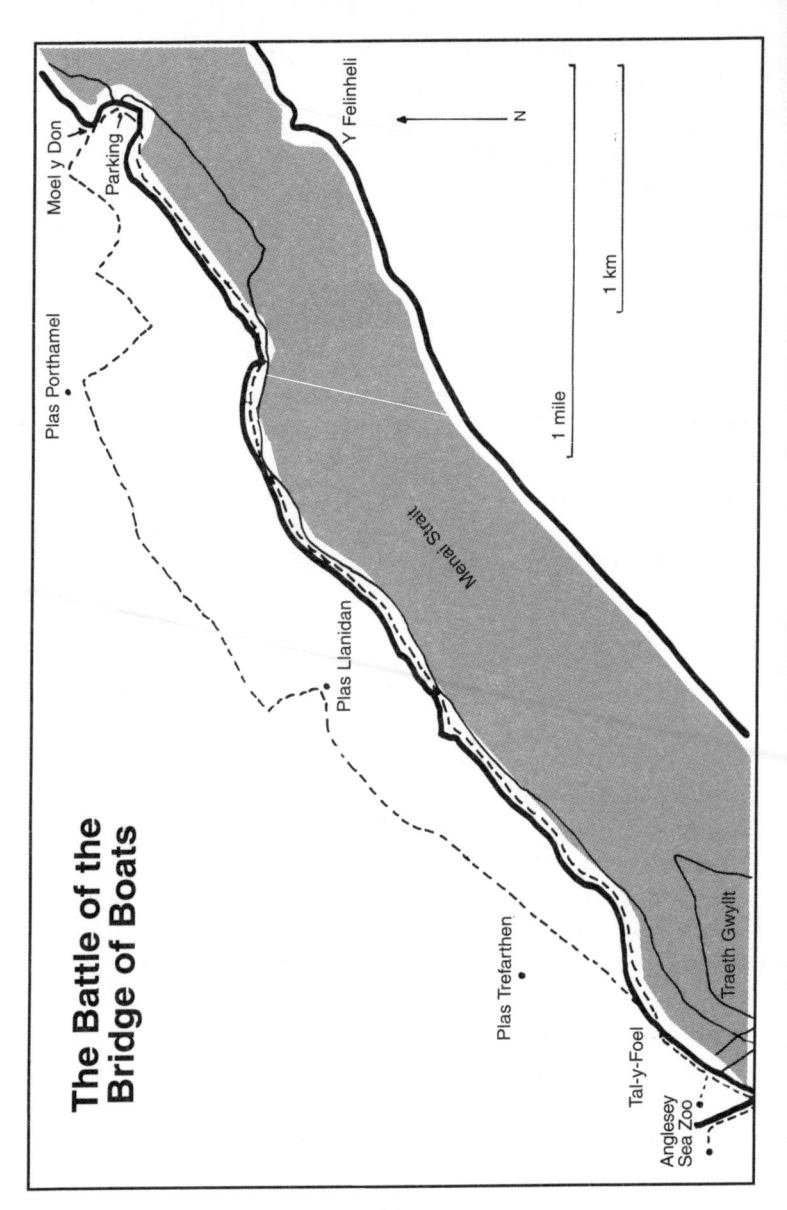

when the tide is out, you can walk on the golden sands rather than on the pebbly beach which is much more difficult to walk on.

If you travel by car, go along the A4080 from Llanfairpwll, past Plas Newydd to the end of the wall until you see the sign to Moel y Don. Go down the road until you reach a parking space by the water's edge.

If travelling by bus, you can go down by the Moel y Don sign and then walk about a mile to the water's edge. Or you can catch a bus to Tal y Foel and start the journey from there, going through the fields first and then returning along the shores of the Strait.

Starting from Moel y Don, go down to the water's edge, turn right and walk along the shore. On the other side of the Strait, you will see Y Felinheli and further along Plas Llanfair, the Water Sports Centre at Plas Menai and the Friction Dynamics factory where the workers were on strike for over two years.

After about an hour's walking along the shore, you will come to a cottage and a road running along the shore. Go onto this road and you will reach the Sea Zoo and Foel Farm with its Chocolate Shop. It is worth calling at these two attractions, if only for a short break and a drink. The Sea Zoo is open all year, but Foel Farm only from March to October. Between these two places are information boards giving details of Traeth Mawr which is in the sea in front of you, and the former ferry over to Caernarfon.

After a rest, go back along the road and onto the beach. Look for a footpath sign and stile on your left. Go over it into the field. Turn right and walk along the field to a small gate. Plas Trefarthen is the large mansion on your left. On this site, about the first century BC, there was a battle between the Romans and the Britons.

Walk along the field that is nearest to the mansion (not the one which is near the Strait) and aim for a stile over a fence. Then to a gate and stile. Then, walk straight across the field to a gate with a stone stile to its right. Here you will see a pole with a yellow sign on it showing you in which direction to go.

Walk along the side of the wall to another gate and stone stile, and then go straight past the trees and into the forest. You might see some pheasants here. Go out of the forest and aim for another stone stile. Over it and then walk diagonally across the field to another gate and stone stile. You are now near Llanidan Farm. Turn right and go down the lane towards Plas Llanidan where you will see peacocks in the garden.

Turn left and walk along the lane with beautiful trees each side of it. Then turn right near a public footpath sign and walk towards a house called Bryn Llwyd. At the junction, go straight ahead, not right, and along an old trackway.

At the next junction, turn right and go past Plas Porthamel and its duck pond. Then turn right and walk along the road. At the next junction, turn left. Near Bron Menai follow the road to the right until you come to another junction. Turn right and go down the hill to Moel y Don (or if you have walked from the main road, turn left to return).

DID YOU SEE THESE?

1. On the map on the information board, where is the furthest point from Moel y Don?

....

2. What is the danger according to the red and yellow sign on the beach?

   ....

3. What is the name of the last cottage on the beach before reaching the road?

   ....

4. What creature is to be found on the Anglesey Sea Zoo sign?

   ....

5. The information board on Traeth Gwyllt mentions an important person who was born in Foel Farm. Who was he?

   ....

6. What is to be found on the two gates leading to Tŷ Llanidan?

   ....

7. Who built the red hay shed in Plas Porthamel?

   ....

8. What was the job of the one living in the cottage by the water in Moel y Don?

   ....

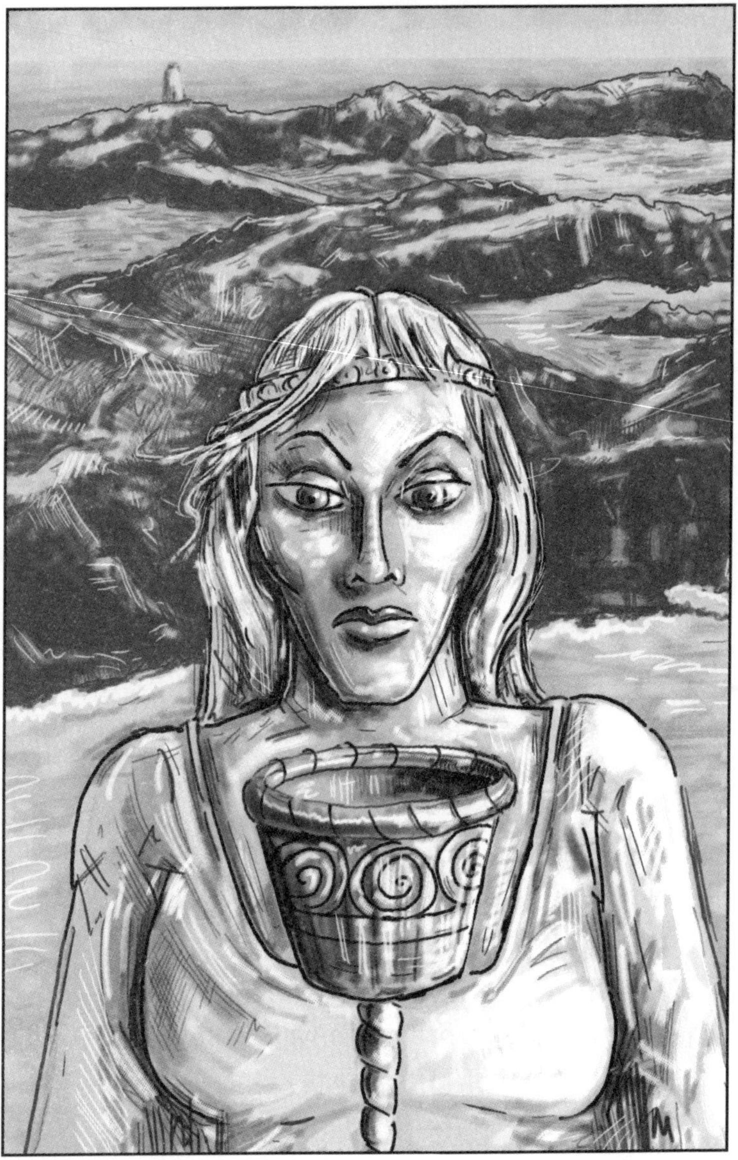

Saint Dwynwen – Patron Saint of Welsh Lovers

THE STORY

Llanddwyn, The Island of Lovers, is on the western coast of Anglesey, but it is not a proper island; it is a promontory sticking out into the sea. But at high tide the sea cuts Llanddwyn from the beach and it becomes an island for a short while.

During the middle of the fifth century a boat landed on Llanddwyn beach. In it were three young people – two sisters and a brother. They had been carried by the waves to Anglesey from south Wales.

The three were the sisters Dwyn and Chain and their brother Dyfan. They had been living with their father, King Brychan, in a large palace – a palace which was full of music, laughter and dancing. One day, their father held a feast there and amongst those that had been invited was a prince called Maelon Dafodrill. Dwyn fell in love with Maelon, and he also fell in love with her.

During the feast, it was announced that they had been engaged. Maelon could not wait to be married and he asked Dwyn to return with him to live in his mansion before the wedding. But she refused as this would have brought shame on her family.

Maelon was very angry and he left the feast in a rage.

Dwyn was very worried about him and followed him into the forest although it was night and very dark. But she could not find him and she started praying hard, so hard that she nearly fainted. Then, in a dream God appeared and offered her a drink. She took the drink and immediately felt better. Also in the dream, she saw Maelon accepting the same drink. But he did not feel better, he turned into a block of ice!

Then God offered Dwyn three wishes. She asked for Maelon to be thawed, for God to listen to her prayers on behalf of other lovers, and that she should never marry anyone.

She went home and told her brother and sister what had happened, and all three decided that they would work for God. The three found a small boat, went into it and left the wind and the waves to carry them far away from home. And that is how they reached Anglesey.

The three built churches on the island – Dwyn in Llanddwyn (*llan* being Welsh for church), Cain in Llangeinwen and Dyfan in Llanddyfnan. These churches were originally built of earth and wood, later replaced by stone buildings. Since Dwyn did many good things for people she was called Dwynwen (Dwyn the Good). Many women came to live on Llanddwyn Island and a convent was built here.

Dwynwen died on 25th January 465, and the 25th of January is known throughout Wales as Saint Dwynwen's Day, similar to the English Saint Valentine's Day. When Dwynwen was about to die, she asked the nuns to carry her outside so that she could see the sun rise for the last time. She was taken to a rock in the north-west corner of the island. Suddenly, so that she could have a better view of the sun, there appeared a huge crack in the rock. And this crack can still be seen there today. At one time, it is believed that there was a well here.

The nuns in the convent continued with their good work after Dwynwen died and by the 14th century there was an important priory here with many visiting the place – especially lovers. In the priory, there was a golden statue of Dwynwen and pilgrims would place lighted candles at the foot of the statue whilst praying. They would also bring small white stones to be placed near the statue.

At one time, about two miles from Llanddwyn, in the dunes of Tywyn Niwbwrch, there was a well called Crochan Llanddwyn (the Llanddwyn cauldron). About a 150 years ago, there was a small cottage near it where lived an old woman who claimed to be able to foretell the future by watching eels in the well. Those that went there looking for a lover would place a handkerchief on the surface of the water which would attract the eels to it. The old woman would watch the eels, and by watching the direction they came from she could tell in which direction the one which had placed the handkerchief would find a lover.

By today, Saint Dwynwen's church is a ruin, but a service is held there once each summer. Towards the end of the 19th century, a cross was placed on the island to remember Saint Dwynwen and her good works.

THE WALK

Along Llanddwyn beach to Llanddwyn Island and back through the forest.
6 miles – 2 hours
Since the bus only goes to Newborough and not to

Saint Dwynwen –
Patron Saint of Welsh Lovers

Newborough Forest

Newborough

Parking

Llanddwyn Beach

Llanddwyn Island

N

1 mile

1 km

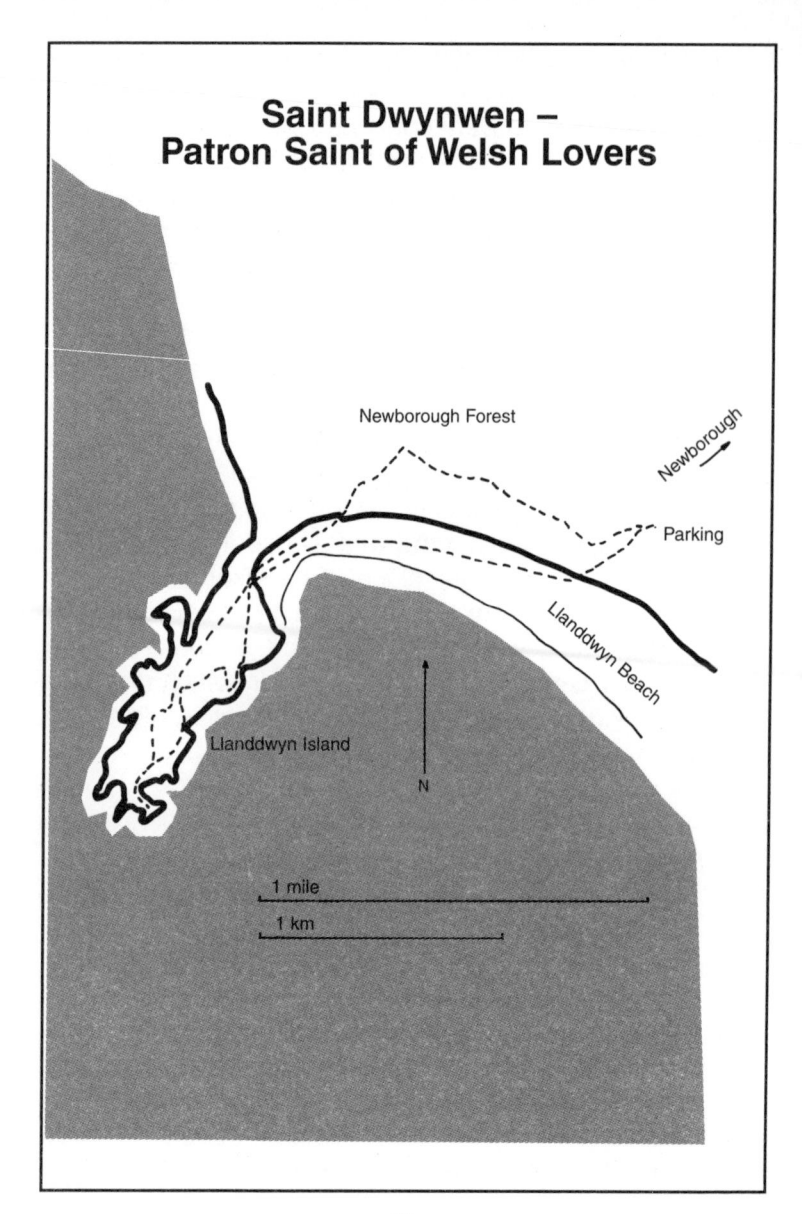

Llanddwyn beach, you will either have to use a car or a bike to reach the starting point of this walk. Follow the signs to 'Llanddwyn' from Newborough. If coming by car, you will have to pay to come to the car park by the beach. Walkers and cyclists do not have to pay. Go through the forest and into the car park where there are toilets and information signs about Llanddwyn beach.

From the car park you will see a path going through the dunes to the beach. Go to the beach and turn right and walk along the golden sands to Llanddwyn Island. Before reaching the island, you will see a small shelter with information on the island on it. Follow the path behind it going left. Look towards the rocks on the left and you might see seals basking in the sun.

Walk towards the lighthouse, but before reaching it you will see a large Celtic cross to the left of the path and the ruins of Dwynwen's church on the right. Continue along the path until you reach the Pilots' Cottages. Here there is an exhibition on the wildlife of the island – why not visit it?

Continue along the path and go left towards a small white tower. This used to warn sailors not to come too near the rocks of Llanddwyn Island. Now walk back towards the large white lighthouse. Go up the path and around the lighthouse for a wonderful view of the Snowdonia mountains. Now, go back down the path, and keeping left, go up a small hill towards another cross. This is Saint Dwynwen's Cross.

Continue along the path and back to Llanddwyn beach. After passing two large rocks on the beach, you will see a path on your left which goes into the forest. Why not follow this path rather than go back along the beach? This forest is home to numerous red squirrels – one of the few places where you can see them in Britain.

Beneath this forest are the remains of the old village of Rhosyr. During a huge storm 700 years ago, sand was blown from the beach covering the village and the people had to leave. You can have more information on the old village by visiting the exhibition in Llys Rhosyr at Newborough.

Continue along the path through the forest until you reach a small car park. Then, turn left along the road and then right and back into the trees. Continue along the path, past a picnic area and information board with details of the flowers and plants to be seen in the area.

Keep to the path until you reach a gate and then you will be back in the car park where you started your journey.

DID YOU SEE THESE?

1. On your way down to the car park you will see humps in the road with small green poles near them. Pictures of what can be seen on these poles?

   ....

2. On the information board in the car park, how many paths are there and what are their colours?

   ....

3. There is a sign by the path to the beach. What does it say that the dunes do?

   ....

4. There is some poetry on the information board before reaching Llanddwyn Island. Who is the poet?

   ....

5. What is in front of the Pilots' Cottages?

   ....

6. When was Saint Dwynwen's Cross erected?

   ....

7. What type of trees are in the forests?

   ....

8. How many types of different flowers and plants can be seen in the sand dunes according to the information board by the picnic area?

   ....

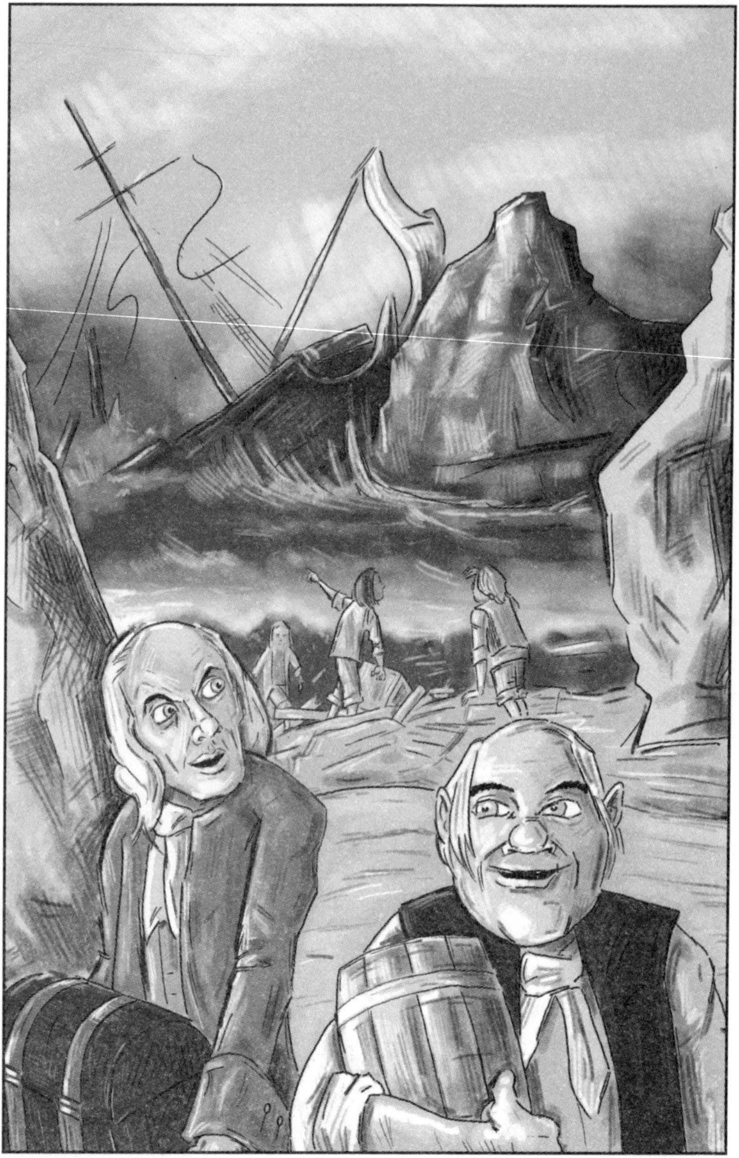

The Wreckers of Crigyll

THE STORY

The coast of Anglesey is a very dangerous place for ships. There are jagged rocks on the coastline and dangerous sandbanks close to the surface, and during stormy weather ships can be blown onto the shore. Two centuries ago, there were people who were more than happy to see ships being blown onto the beaches so that they could steal their cargoes.

There was such a group of people living near Traeth Crigyll in Rhosneigr. It is said that the Wreckers of Crigyll would wave their lamps on the beach so that ships thought it was safe to come ashore. Traeth Crigyll was a good place for the wreckers to live. There were rocks offshore and lots of sand dunes where they could hide, as well as frequent mists to hide their evil deeds.

One stormy night in December 1741, a ship called Loveday and Betty was sailing off the coast of Anglesey. But the following morning she was thrown onto the rocks near the mouth of the river Crigyll. She had not suffered much damage, apart from scraping her keel on the rocks.

Captain Jackson from Liverpool made sure that his ship was safely anchored and then went to fetch help to get the ship back into the water. But news of the ship on the shore quickly spread throughout the area, and after it got dark ten local men went to the beach. They first took the sails, then the ropes and carried them to the horses that were waiting in the dunes to carry them away.

When the captain returned, he saw that there were many things missing from his ship and he decided to go to Aberffraw to look for the customs officer to report the theft. Both returned to Traeth Crigyll on horseback and decided to follow the tracks of the wreckers through the sand dunes. They galloped after the wreckers and eventually caught up with them and captured four of them.

On 7th April 1741, the wreckers were tried in the court in Beaumaris. There was a great deal of interest in the case, and many people travelled from afar to see the trial, hoping that all four would be hanged. But the judge was drunk and he decided to free the four wreckers!

Before then, in April 1715, three of the Crigyll Wreckers had been brought to court for stealing goods from a ship called The Charming Jenny which had also been blown onto the beach. These were not so fortunate – they were all hanged. This was the first time that people had heard of the Wreckers of Crigyll.

The stealing continued for another century. There was one famous case towards the end of October 1867 when goods were stolen from a ship called Earl of Chester. According to a report in The Times newspaper, "there were hundreds of them carrying everything from the ship".

But by today, Traeth Crigyll is a very peaceful place with sailing boats and children building sand castles where once wreckers lurked waiting for ships to go on the rocks.

THE WALK

From Rhosneigr across the sands of Traeth Crigyll and back through Tywyn Traean past RAF Valley and back to

Rhosneigr.
5 miles – 2 hours
Park your car in the free car park near the library and toilets in Rhosneigr and then walk down the hill. Turn right and then go along the main street. If you are travelling by bus, there is a bus stop here. Walk towards the war memorial with the clock on top.

Then turn left and go down the hill to the beach. Turn right and walk along the sands until you come to the mouth of the Crigyll river. You will have to take your shoes and socks off to cross it. If you don't want to get your feet wet, walk up river to a footbridge and then return to the beach. The vast stretch of sand ahead of you is Traeth Crigyll where the wreckers carried out their evil deeds.

Walk to the far end of Traeth Crigyll; around the corner is Traeth Cymyran (where Madam Wen's ship was anchored – see Story No. 4). Walk for a few yards on Traeth Cymyran, but then look for a path that goes up into the dunes. Go up into the dunes and before you is RAF Valley with its hangars and landing strips. It is possible that you will see aircraft landing and taking off, and it is quite possible that you will have heard them in the skies after reaching Rhosneigr.

Look for a small fence that goes across Tywyn Trewan. Every tenth pole has been painted red and white and there are signs warning you not to go onto the airfield land. Follow the path that runs alongside the fence.

Then, near a high fence and cabins, the fence – and path – turns right. Follow this path and although it turns left further along, walk straight ahead aiming for the footbridge. Go over the footbridge and up the lane to a cluster of houses. The lane goes past the houses and takes you to a large square building. Turn left near this

The Wreckers of Crigyll

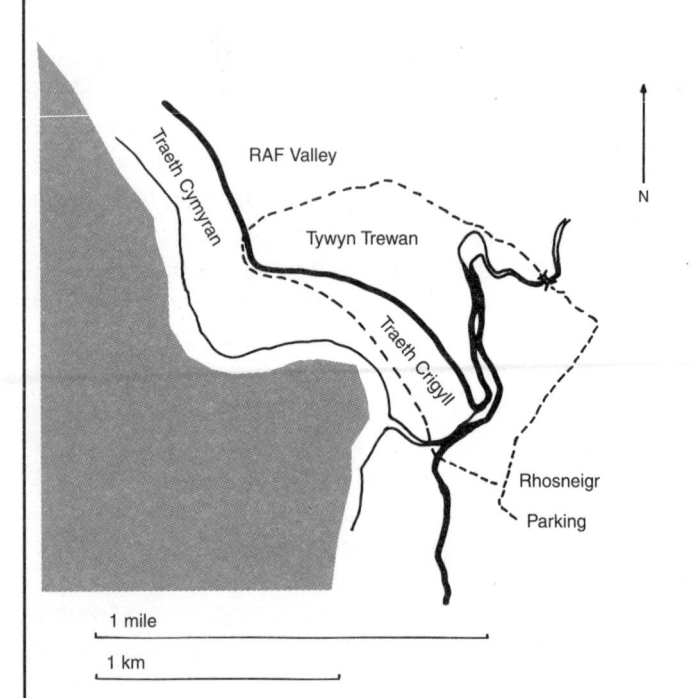

building and then into the main road. Turn right and walk back into the village.

HAVE YOU SEE THESE?

1. What are the opening times of the library on Saturday?

   ....

2. On the cenotaph, who was the first to be killed during the Second World War?

   ....

3. According to Ynys Môn Council, what can't you do with a vehicle on Traeth Crigyll?

   ....

4. Who, according to the sign on the fence, owns the land that you are prohibited from going on?

   ....

5. What is the name of the road that leads back into the village?

   ....

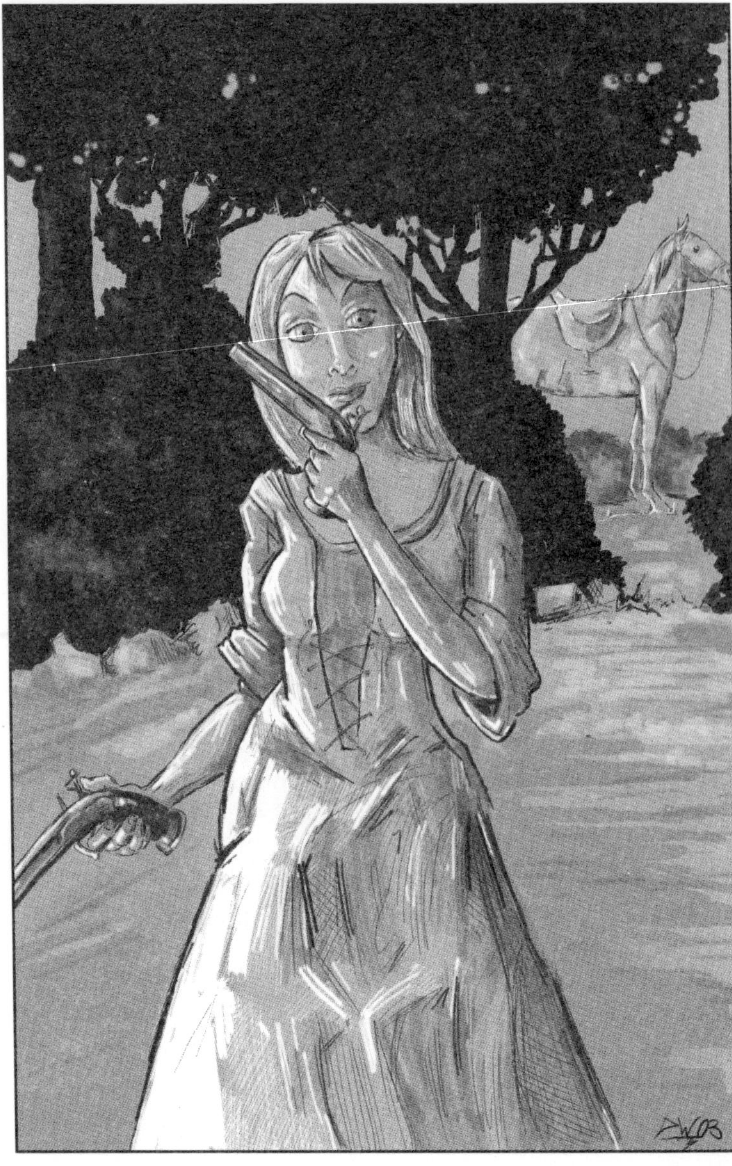

Madam Wen – the Welsh Highwaywoman

THE STORY

Madam Wen lived in the lakes district of west Anglesey in the 18th century. Einir Wyn was her real name and she came from a family that were at one time wealthy and owned a lot of land. But during the English Civil War (1642-1651), the family lost much of their lands because they had supported the King against Parliament.

But Madam Wen was determined to get some money to buy these lands back. She gathered together a gang of men who went robbing and smuggling on Anglesey. Madam Wen had one of the best horses on Anglesey and could outrun everyone, and she only travelled at night galloping as fast as her horse could take her.

The authorities did not know who was responsible for all the robberies and smuggling on the island and when they did come across Madam Wen they could not catch her. Madam Wen and her gang used to hide in a cave near Llyn Traffwll and since the entrance was hidden by very thick and high gorse bushes it was impossible to find them.

One night, with snow thick on the ground, Madam Wen and her gang went to hold up the stagecoach. But the authorities were watching the coach and they galloped after Madam Wen and her gang. They were determined to catch her, but one of the gang, Wil the blacksmith, had a brainwave. He took the horseshoes off Madam Wen's horse and put them back on back-to-front. The authorities, rather than following Madam Wen's horse tracks in the snow, were going in the direction that she had come from!

Madam Wen and her gang would also smuggle goods into Anglesey. It is said that she had a ship anchored off Cymyran Bay, and her gang would carry the smuggled goods to be sold all over the island. As people were not paying taxes on these goods, the authorities were very angry and they were very keen to catch Madam Wen – but they always failed.

Only one member of the gang was ever caught – Wil the blacksmith. He had gone to Menai Bridge fair and was about to start off home when he put someone else's saddle on his horse in mistake. He was accused of stealing the saddle and dragged to the court, found guilty and fined. Wil was so embarrassed by being caught for something so petty, and he having stolen so much over the years, that he emigrated to America to live!

But Madam Wen did eventually become the owner of much land – but not her family's lands. Einir Wyn married Morris Williams, owner of the Cymunod estate, and both lived happily ever after with very few people knowing that she had been Madam Wen.

Some people say that they have seen the ghost of Madam Wen in the lakes, especially on Easter Sunday morning. It is said that she swims backwards and forwards and then when she reaches the middle, she disappears!

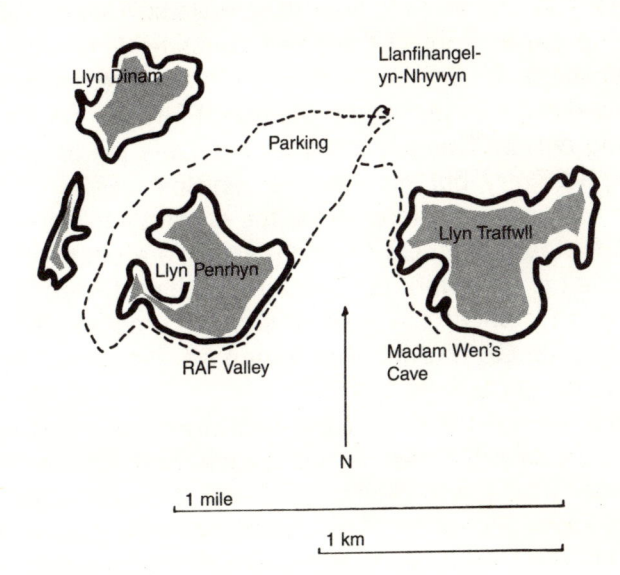

Madam Wen – The Welsh Highwaywoman

THE WALK

From Llanfihangel-yn-Nhywyn, between Dinam and Penrhyn lakes, past RAF Valley and back to Llanfihangel-yn-Nhywyn. Then, if you have enough time, why not go and look for Madam Wen's cave?

The walk can be a bit wet after heavy rain; it might therefore be a good idea to take wellingtons with you.

4 miles – 1½ hours (+ ½ hour to visit Madam Wen's cave)

Park the car in front of the shop opposite St Mihangel's Church in Llanfihangel-yn-Nhywyn, or if you are coming by bus there is a bus stop nearby. Go into Ffordd Cerrig Mawr housing estate. There is a Ministry of Defence sign here saying No Entry, but this refers to vehicles only.

Go through the estate and at the far end you will see a public footpath sign. Go down the track to a small house. To the left is a kissing gate, go through it and keep to the right hand side of the field until you come to another kissing gate. Go through it and then go straight ahead – don't turn right.

Then, at the far end of the field, turn right and walk towards a stile. Go over it and across the next field to a stile near a gate. Go over it and follow the path with Llyn Penrhyn on your left until you come to another stile near a gate. Go over it and along the field with the lake and rock to your left. If you climb to the top of the rock, you will see Llyn Dinam on the right.

Look for a pole with a yellow arrow on it behind clumps of gorse. There is a path near it; turn left and then go over a bridge made of wooden planks and on to another one. Follow the path between two rocks, keeping to the left or go over one of the rocks if it is too wet and then follow the path through the gorse.

You will then come to a footbridge, go over it and follow the path until you come to three poles with lamps on them on your right. The path goes past the third pole and then you will see more lamps on your left. You will then come to a track and then to a row of lamps on a fence.

Walk towards a gate and stile, go through the gate and continue along the path to the Valley Lakes Nature Reserve car park. Go out of the car park near the RAF Valley entrance and then turn left, walking along the pavement back to Llanfihangel-yn-Nhywyn where the journey started.

Madam Wen's Cave is near Llyn Traffwll – why not try and find it? On the way back to Llanfihangel-yn-Nhywyn after passing RAF Valley, you will see Bryn Trewan housing estate on your right. Turn into the estate and walk until you come to a junction. Turn right and go down a narrow lane. Before you come to an agricultural building, you will see a muddy track going towards a gate. In the corner, near a tree, there is an old stile on the right (it is a bit difficult to find).

Go over the stile and across the field, aiming for a gate in the far end. To the left of the gate is an iron stile. You will now see Llyn Traffwll to the left and some large rocks in front of you. Somewhere in these rocks is Madam Wen's Cave. Go over the stile and walk along the shore of the lake through the rocks and gorse bushes until you come to a flat field on the lake shore. Before reaching this field, there is a large rock with a huge crack in it. This is Madam Wen's Cave. Some say that there is a secret room beneath it. Can you find it?

CAN YOU ANSWER THESE?

1. Who worships in St Mihangel's Church?

   ....

2. Near the entrance to Ffordd Cerrig Mawr estate, a red sign mentions children. What does it say?

   ....

3. How many lamps are there on the fence before you reach the nature reserve car park?

   ....

4. The RSPB sign says that there are three types of ducks in the reserve. What are they?

   ....

   ....

   ....

5. How far is the airfield guardroom according to the sign in the RAF Valley entrance?

   ....

6. There are two telephone kiosks near the Spar shop. What are their phone numbers?

   ....

7. What is the name of the small whitewashed cottage by the side of the road before reaching the Llanfihangel-yn-Nhywyn sign?

   ....

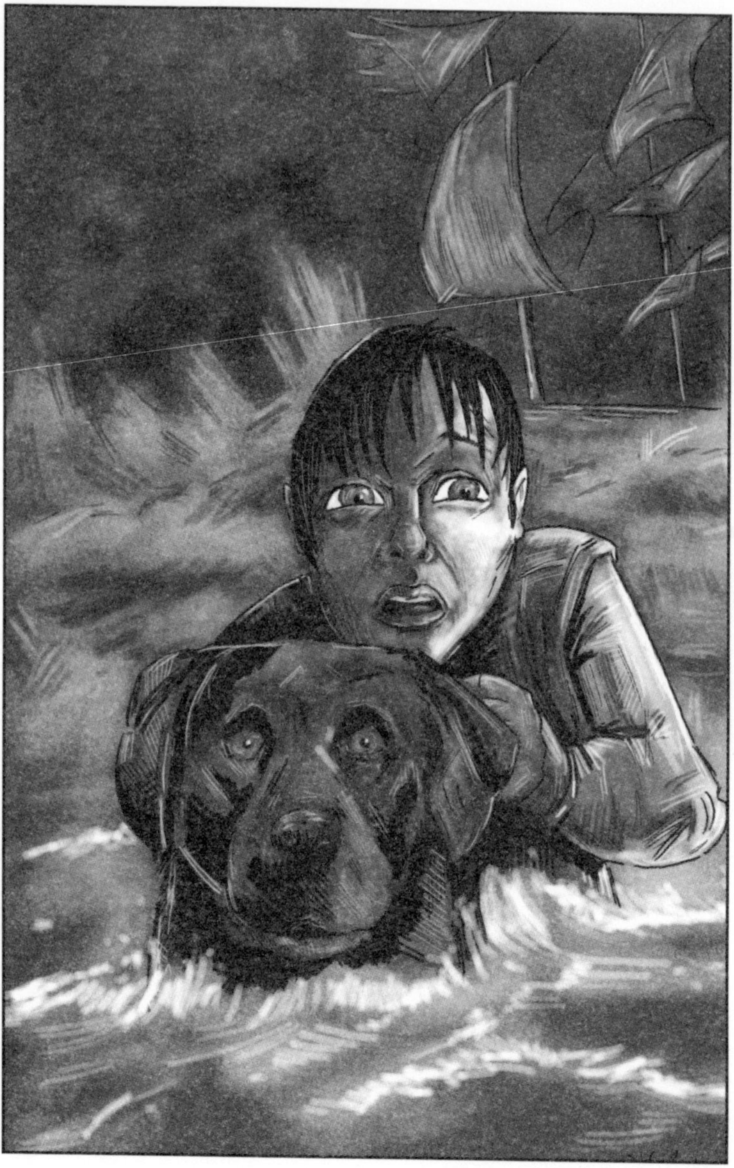

Tyger the Brave Dog

THE STORY

Nearly two hundred years ago, a small ship was sailing along the western coast of Anglesey on its way to Liverpool. On board were the captain, two sailors, a cabin boy and a retriever called Tyger. There was a thick mist and the captain was not sure where exactly he was.

Suddenly, there was a loud bang. The ship had hit the rocks of Maen Pisgar, a small island about three quarters of a mile offshore. As the ship was not sinking, nothing could be done, so the captain decided to wait for the mist to lift.

The tide came in and lifted the ship off the rocks, but as there was a hole in its keel, the water started to flow in, and the ship started to sink. The thick mist was around them and the crew were not sure in which direction to swim for the shore.

Tyger had also realised that they were in danger. But he knew in which direction the coast was and he jumped into the sea and started swimming. The captain decided that the crew should follow Tyger and they all jumped into the sea.

The captain was a strong swimmer, but the others weren't. The cabin boy grabbed hold of Tyger's collar and he was dragged slowly to the pebbly beach. The captain then realised that one of the sailors was in difficulty, so after Tyger had left the cabin boy safely on the beach, he

Tyger the Brave Dog

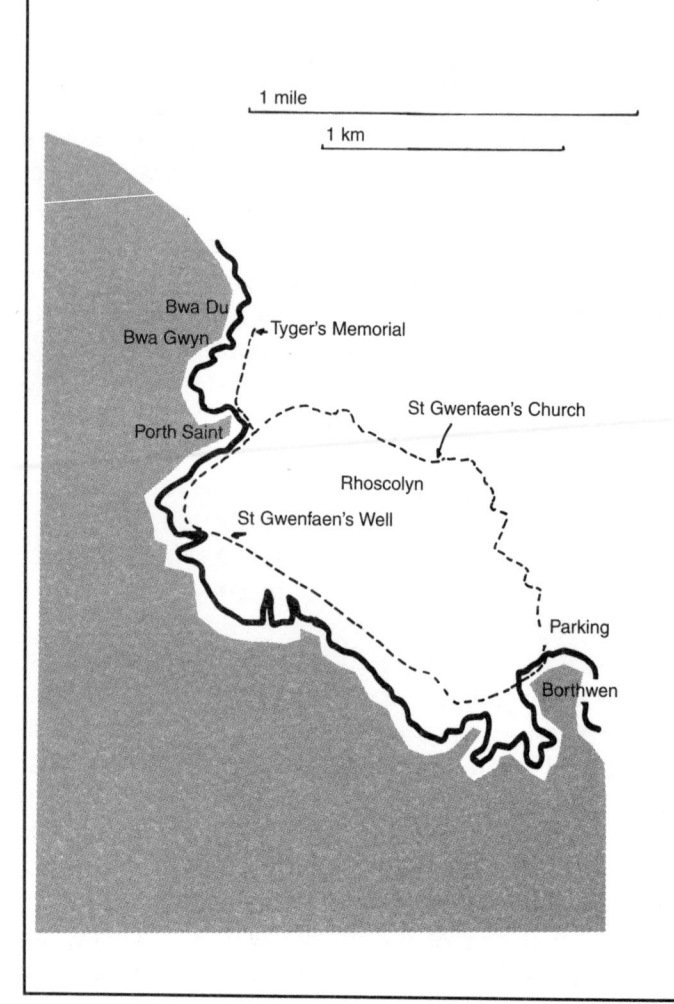

asked Tyger to return to help the sailor.

Tyger returned and grabbed hold of the sailor's collar with his teeth and dragged him to the shore. The dog then returned to help the other sailor and then his master, the captain.

All five lay very tired and wet on the beach. One by one, they got up – but not Tyger. He was too tired. He raised his head and licked the captain's hand before dying on the cold, wet beach.

If it had not been for Tyger's bravery, they would have all drowned. And in order to show his appreciation of his brave dog, the captain paid for a stone to be placed on the cliff above the beach where all four landed safely and where Tyger had died.

And the stone is still there, and on it the words: Tyger, September 17th, 1819.

THE WALK

From Borthwen beach near Rhoscolyn along the shore, past St Gwenfaen's Well, to Tyger's memorial stone, and back along an inland route to Borthwen.
5 miles – 2 hours

Go to the village of Rhoscolyn and look for the church. About a hundred feet to the west of the church you will see a sign to the beach. It is possible to reach Rhoscolyn by bus, but you will then have to walk to the church and start your walk from here. Go down to the beach where there is a car park and toilets. It can be very full here in summer, and you may find parking space by the church; you can then start the walk from there.

At Borthwen, walk to the right to a concrete wall and

path. Follow the path which brings you back to the beach. Then go past the old lifeboat house. Go up the hill to the white house where you will see yellow signs pointing to the right towards a house called Yr Allt.

Then go straight ahead along the shore, past the coastguard look-out station on your left and another look-out and bench on your right. After a while you will reach St Gwenfaen's Well, where, they say, if you throw two white stones into its waters, you will be cured of any mental illness.

Carry on along the path, through a kissing gate, and along the path that runs alongside a high wall. You will then reach Porth Saint. Cross the small footbridge and continue along the path. Now, you should see a large white house in front of you; there is no need for you to go as far as there. After you pass a small bay, you will see five stones on your left. The first of these is Tyger's memorial stone. When the tide is out, you can see Maen Pisgar out at sea where the ship was wrecked.

After a rest, turn back for Porth Saint. To the left you will see a stile, go over it and along the field to another stile. Then follow the old track until you reach the farmhouse. Follow the yellow signs around the house until you come to a kissing gate and public footpath sign. Go through the gate, then to the left and along the road until you reach St Gwenfaen's Church. Why not go and see the church? Then look for the sign to the beach. Walk down the road, past the pub, and along the winding road back to the car park.

DID YOU SEE THESE?

1. What is not allowed in the car park?

   ....

2. What is the date on the old lifeboat station?

   ....

3. How many seats are there in the corners of St Gwenfaen's Well?

   ....

4. What are the letters in the concrete near the kissing gate after going past St Gwenfaen's Well?

   ....

5. Which two disciples of Jesus Christ are shown on the stained-glass windows of St Gwenfaen's Church porch?

   ....

6. After which bird has the pub on the way down to the beach been named?

   ....

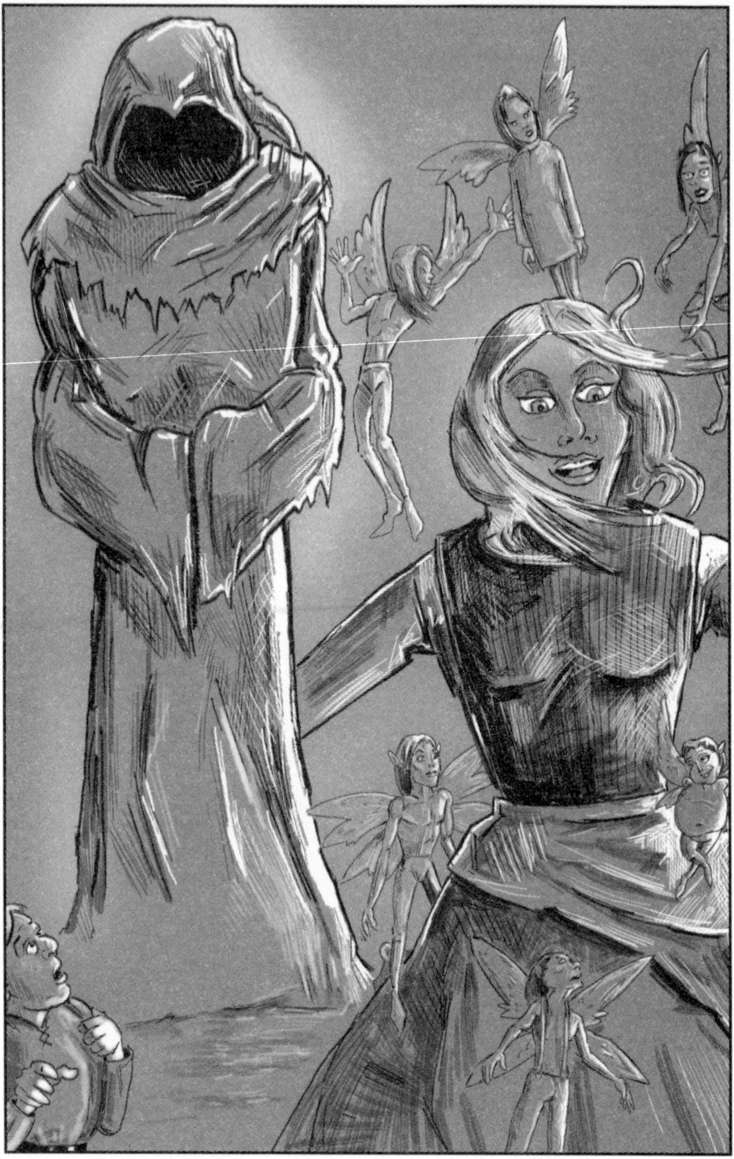

The Thief of Dyfrydog and the girl amongst the Fairies

THE STORY OF THE THIEF OF DYFRYDOG

We will start with the story of the Thief of Dyfrydog. In St Tyfrydog's Church at one time, as in all other churches on Anglesey, there was a large Bible and Prayer Book tied to the pulpit with a chain in case someone tried to steal them.

At one time, a man called Wil Llaw Flewog would go to the church to read the two books, but one day he decided to steal them. He broke the chain, and took a red cloth from the altar and wrapped the two books along with the communion vessels in it. He then ran out of the church towards Clorach farm.

But as he was running across Clorach fields, the ghost of a monk stood in front of him. The monk was as tall as an oak tree and when he walked the ground would shake as if there was an earthquake.

"Who are you?" asked Wil. And these were the last words that came from Wil Llaw Flewog's mouth before he was turned into stone.

And the stone is still there today, with Wil and his bundle on his back and his mouth half open. According to tradition, every time the clock strikes seven, Wil runs wildly around the field!

THE STORY OF IFAN GRUFFUDD'S DAUGHTER

Ifan Gruffudd and his daughter Gwen lived on Hafod Isaf farm near Llandyfrydog nearly two hundred years ago. One Christmas day, Gwen had promised to go to another farm, Hafod Uchaf, to see some friends, to sing, dance and tell stories.

She was about to start when her father asked her to go and fetch the cow and take it to the cow shed before it got dark. But there was no sign of the cow, even through Gwen looked everywhere. So, she went back into the house to tell her father. Then both of them went out to try and find the cow, but it was still missing. They eventually reached the field where the Thief of Dyfrydog stone is today.

In the middle of the field, they saw fairies dancing in a circle. They were wearing clothes of the seven colours of the rainbow and they were spinning around and around on the grass. Suddenly, Gwen jumped into the fairy circle, and then disappeared. Ifan Gruffudd was left on his own in The Thief of Dyfrydog field on Christmas night!

He went home and told all the neighbours what had happened, and within a few hours everyone in Llandyfrydog had learnt of what had happened to Gwen. Within a few days, everyone on Anglesey had heard that she had disappeared into the fairy circle.

Weeks and months went by, and still there was no sign of Gwen. Many believed that Ifan Gruffudd would never see his daughter again.

But Ifan Gruffudd remembered that a wizard lived near

Maenaddwyn, and he decided to visit him. John Roberts the wizard lived in a small cottage on the slopes of Mynydd Bodafon. When he arrived at the small cottage, Ifan Gruffudd told the story of his missing daughter.

"If you want your daughter back," said the wizard, "go back to the same field next Christmas night – at exactly the same time as your daughter disappeared into the fairy circle. You will have to take with you the four strongest men in the area to help you. You must also buy a very strong rope. All five of you will have to be in the field at the right time. Tie the rope around your waist, and when you see Gwen dancing in the fairy circle, jump in and pull her out."

Ifan Gruffudd went looking for the four strongest men in the area, and each one was more than happy to help him. At that time, many people in nearby Llannerch-y-medd were experts at rope-making, and Ifan Gruffudd paid them a visit and asked them to make him a very strong rope.

Christmas Day, after tea, Ifan Gruffudd and the four strong men went into the Thief of Dyfrydog field. The moon rose above the trees, and suddenly Gwen and the fairies appeared, dancing in the middle of the field. Ifan Gruffudd tied the rope around his waist with the biggest knot anyone had seen. The four strong men held the other end as tight as they could. Suddenly, Ifan Gruffudd jumped into the fairy circle and grabbed Gwen.

"Pull! Pull!" he shouted as loud as he could. The four strong men started to pull on the rope, and eventually Ifan and his daughter Gwen were pulled free from the fairy circle. "Where's the cow?" asked Gwen when she was safe out of the circle. She had not realised that she had disappeared with the fairies for a full year.

By now the fairies had disappeared and everyone went home happily, especially Ifan Gruffudd who had got his

The Thief of Dyfrydog and the girl amongst the Fairies

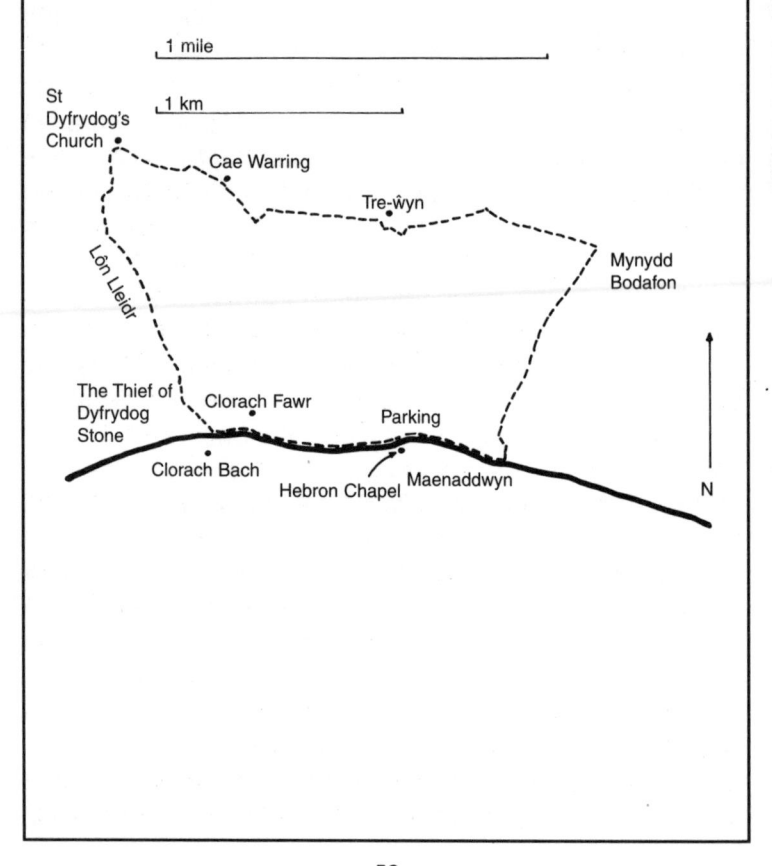

daughter Gwen back from the fairies.

THE WALK

From Maenaddwyn past Mynydd Bodafon, towards St Dyfrydog's Church, past Clorach and back to Maenaddwyn.
4 miles – 1½ hours

Park your car in Maenaddwyn in front of the houses opposite Hebron chapel. Buses travel along this road and you can ask the driver to drop you off here. Walk carefully along the road in the direction of Benllech until you come to a crossroads. Turn left and walk along the narrow road.

You will then come to a T-junction. In front of you is a gate; go through it and walk across the field with Mynydd Bodafon to your right until you reach a gate and stone stile. Over the stile and then to your left and walk along the edge of the field to the corner. There is a stone stile here but it is impossible to go over it, therefore walk to the right alongside the wall until you come to a large white gate. Through the gate and turn left and walk along the lane to a crossroads.

Turn right and go down the hill until you come to a gate, wooden stile and public footpath sign on the left. Go over the stile into the field and walk alongside the field to the corner and then right and down the edge of the field and then right, walking alongside the wall towards the farm.

When you come to a fence, turn right and walk a few metres to a small stile. Go over the stile and you will see a gate in front of you. Go through the gate and you will arrive at the entrance to Tre-ŵyn farm. Go to your right, past the large shed and through the small gate on the right into the trees. Go through the trees towards a stile. Over the stile and down the field, walking alongside the fence on your left to another stile.

Over the stile and go straight ahead; don't go through the gate on your left but go straight ahead to another stile. Go over it and alongside the edge of the field to the corner where there is a gate. Don't go through the gate, but turn right along the track towards Cae Warring farm.

When you reach a gate and stile, go over the stile, through the farm yard and through a gate. Walk down the farm lane, past the Vicerage on your right and on towards St Dyfrydog's Church. When you reach the road, turn left and walk along Lôn Lleidr (Thief Lane) until you reach a crossroads.

Turn left. Before you reach the next crossroads, in the field on your right is the Thief of Dyfrydog Stone and where the fairies used to dance. Unfortunately, there is no public footpath through the field. Continue to the crossroads with Clorach Bach in front of you. Turn left and walk carefully along the road past Clorach Fawr on the left and back to Hebron chapel and the car or bus.

DID YOU SEE THESE?

1. There are two signs before reaching the crossroads at Maenaddwyn. One is a crossroads sign, the other has a picture on it. A picture of what?

   ....

2. How many Xs are there on the Vicerage gate?

   ....

3. On which Sundays are there services in St Dyfrydog's Church?

   ....

4. What is the building to the left of St Dyfrydog's Church?

   ....

5. On the crossroads near Clorach Bach there is a sign. What is on this sign?

   ....

6. In what year was Hebron chapel opened?

   ....

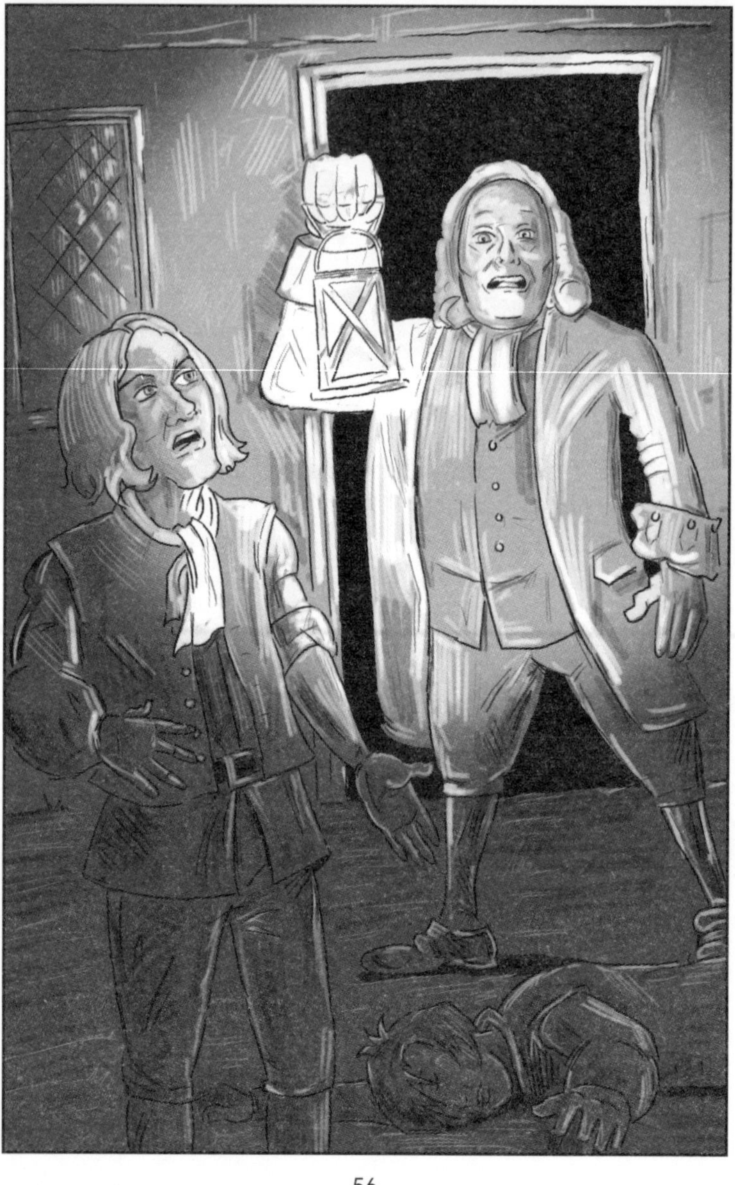

The Bonesetters of Anglesey

THE STORY

One dark, stormy night, during the 18th century, a smuggler pushed his boat into the sea and started rowing for one of the numerous caves on the Anglesey coast. But suddenly, he heard someone shouting "Help!" He could see nothing in the darkness, but started rowing towards the cries.

He then came across a small boat with two boys clutching tightly to it. The smuggler pulled the boys into his boat and started rowing furiously to the shore, but one of the boys had already died before he reached safety. About half a mile from the shore was Mynachdy where Dr Lloyd lived. The smuggler took the boy to him.

Slowly, the boy came round, but they could not find where he had come from because he could speak no Welsh or English. They learnt that he was called Evan or something similar, and in later years the local people though that he might have come from a Spanish ship which had sunk on the Skerries rocks.

Evan stayed with Dr Lloyd and he was given the surname Thomas. One day Dr Lloyd was about to kill one of his hens for Sunday dinner as it had broken one of its legs. But Evan got hold of the hen, set the bones and made a small splint to keep them in place until they mended.

After a while, Evan would accompany Dr Lloyd when he went to see his patients. At first, Evan would mend the broken bones of the patients' animals, but later he was allowed to set the bones of the patients themselves. The story of Evan's skills rapidly spread through Anglesey and people from all over the island came to see him to mend their bones.

And it wasn't only Evan Thomas who had this skill. Every one of his sons could also mend bones. If you go for a walk to Church Bay on the island, you will go past a house called Cilmaenan. There is a plaque on the side of the house saying that a son of Evan Thomas, Richard Evans (1772-1851), had lived there.

One of Evan Thomas's nephews, of the same name as him, opened a surgery in Liverpool and became a wealthy man. He had seven children and one of them, Hugh Owen Thomas, trained to become a doctor. He became famous throughout Britain as an orthopaedic (bone) surgeon, and he devised many things for the medical profession, including the Thomas splint to hold broken bones together.

His nephew, Sir Robert Jones, opened the famous orthopaedic hospital in Gobowen on the Welsh-English border which treats many people from north and mid Wales and the English Midlands.

THE WALK

From Mynachdy near Llanfair-yng-Nghornwy to Hen Borth and Carmel Head and back.

6 miles – 2½ hours
*So that you don't disturb the wildlife, you can only do this walk between 1 February and 14 September.

Go off the A5025 and turn towards Llanfair-yng-Nghornwy. Go through the village until you come to a crossroads. To the right is a sign saying Private Road. Park your car here (there is no bus service).

Walk to your right down the Private Road, past a house on the right and continue to Mynachdy farm where Dr Lloyd lived. Go into the farmyard, and then through the gate on your right, following the track across the field to a gate and stone stile. Over the stile and along the field to a gate. Don't go through the gate but go to the wooden stile on the right.

Over the stile and down the path to Hen Felin. Near the Hen Felin gate there is a footpath sign to your left. Go through the small gate and over the footbridge and through the kissing gate. Walk along the side of the field and you will arrive on the beach at Hen Borth. Turn left and walk between two fences to a gate and kissing gate. Go through the kissing gate and either walk on the beach or on the path above the beach until you come to another kissing gate.

Walk along the coastal path, often above a small cliff. Out in the sea, you will see West Mouse island and the Skerries where Evan Thomas was probably shipwrecked. To your right you will see a Danger sign warning you to keep away from an old mine shaft.

Continue along the path, over the stile, then over a footbridge and follow the path up the slope. Over another footbridge and over two stone stiles.

You will then see the White Ladies. These are white triangular towers – two on the mainland and one on West

The Bonesetters of Anglesey

Mouse. They are in one long line and were used by sea captains to navigate around Carmel Head.

You will now have reached Carmel Head – about half way through the walk. Why not stop here for a picnic? In front of you, there is a tall chimney and if you go towards it you will find the remains of an old copper mine. Copper ore used to be burnt in the furnace under the chimney. It is said that copper was mined here thousands of years ago.

Walk now towards the White Lady furthest from the sea. Then turn left and walk towards a gap in the wall. Walk along the path towards a small forest. Keep to the right of the forest and follow the path between the trees and a rock until you come to a gate and stone stile.

Go over the stile and follow the path to a small lake (this may be dry in summer). Continue to a gate and stile and then down towards a larger lake. Follow the concrete track in front of the dam to another gate and stone stile. Over the stile and continue along the track to another gate and stone stile and back to Mynachdy.

Turn right and the walk back to the car.

DID YOU SEE THESE?

1. On the information sign about Mynachdy near Hen Felin, how many acres of land has the National Trust?

   ....

2. What is the large building you see to the east whilst walking?

   ....

3. What does the sign near Hen Borth tell you to do?

   ....

4. What flashes out at sea?

   ....

5. How many seconds are there between each flash?

   ....

6. What is the name of the farm on the right before you arrive back at the car?

   ....

The sinking of the Royal Charter

THE STORY

During the middle of the 19th century, the Royal Charter was one of the fastest and most luxurious ships in the world. She was built at Sandycroft on the banks of the river Dee in north-east Wales. She could sail from Britain to Australia in 60 days. And that was her main duty – carrying people to the gold fields of Australia and then carrying them back, often having made their fortunes.

On August 26 1859, there were 390 passengers and numerous small boxes full of gold (worth £322,440) on board when the Royal Charter left Melbourne for Britain. Many of the passengers also carried money belts around their waists full of gold pieces. They had fine weather on the journey, and when the ship reached Ireland, the captain promised them that he would again have made the journey within 60 days.

But when they approached the coast of Anglesey, the wind strengthened and the weather got worse. But, rather than looking for shelter, the captain decided to hurry towards Liverpool as he had promised the passengers.

By six o'clock on October 25, the Royal Charter had just gone past the Skerries, when the wind strengthened even more and began blowing the ship towards the shore. The captain fired a distress rocket to try and summon help,

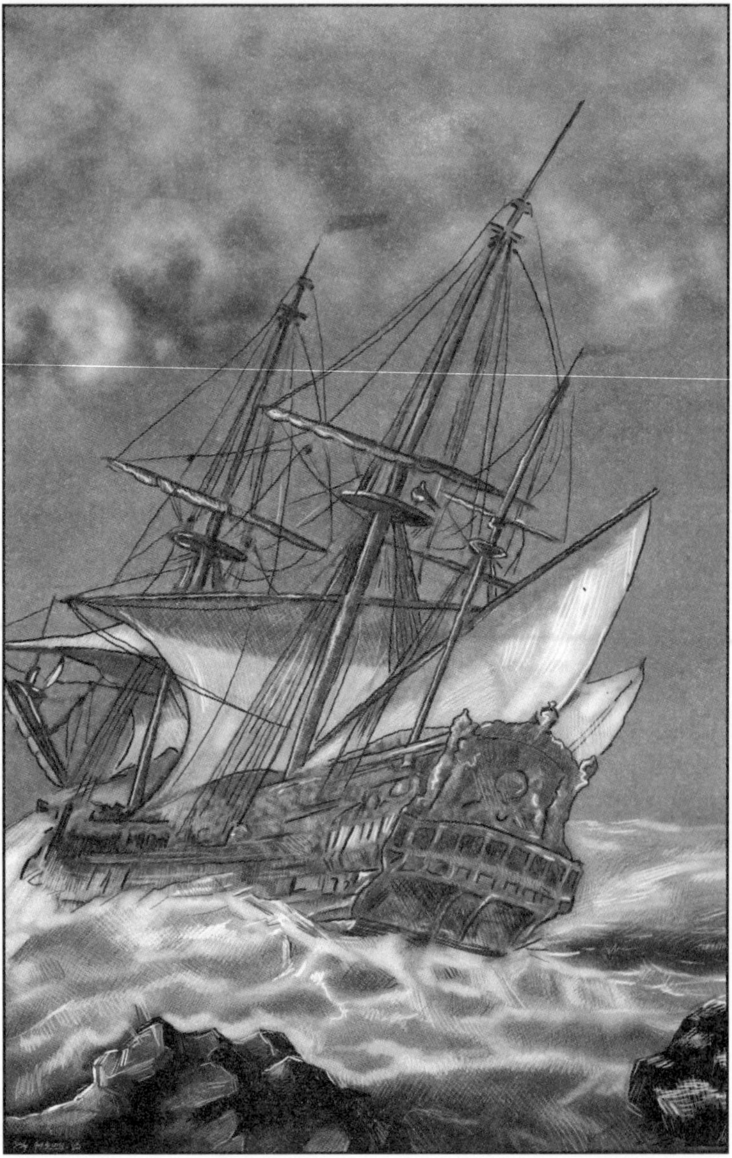

but the weather was too bad for any other ship to try and come to the rescue. The captain then lowered three anchors, but – one by one – the heavy, thick cables broke, such was the strength of the wind blowing the ship towards the shore.

The passengers – men, women and children – were very frightened, and the captain came on deck to reassure them and to tell them that the ship was near the shore and that they would be rescued in the morning. And when dawn broke, everyone saw that they were only 23 metres from the shore. But there were huge waves between them and land, some as high as 20 metres.

One brave sailor offered to swim to the shore with a rope around his waist to take it to the people that had gathered on the beach to try and help the passengers. The sailor reached the beach and a small chair was tied to the rope. People were put one by one on the chair and pulled to safety.

But at seven o'clock, there was a huge bang and the Royal Charter broke in half. The passengers and crew were thrown into the foaming sea and some were crushed by the broken timbers of the ship. The sea was too stormy for anyone to try to rescue the people in the water.

Of the 490 people, including the crew, only 38 managed to reach the shore safely, and none of the children or women were rescued. Four hundred and sixty-two people lost their lives, and their bodies were kept in Llanallgo church until they were buried in the cemetery. People from all over Britain came to Anglesey to see if their relatives were among the dead. Many reporters, also, came to the area to write stories for the newspapers about the awful tragedy, and amongst them was the famous author Charles Dickens.

About £300,000 worth of gold from the ship was found,

The sinking of the *Royal Charter*

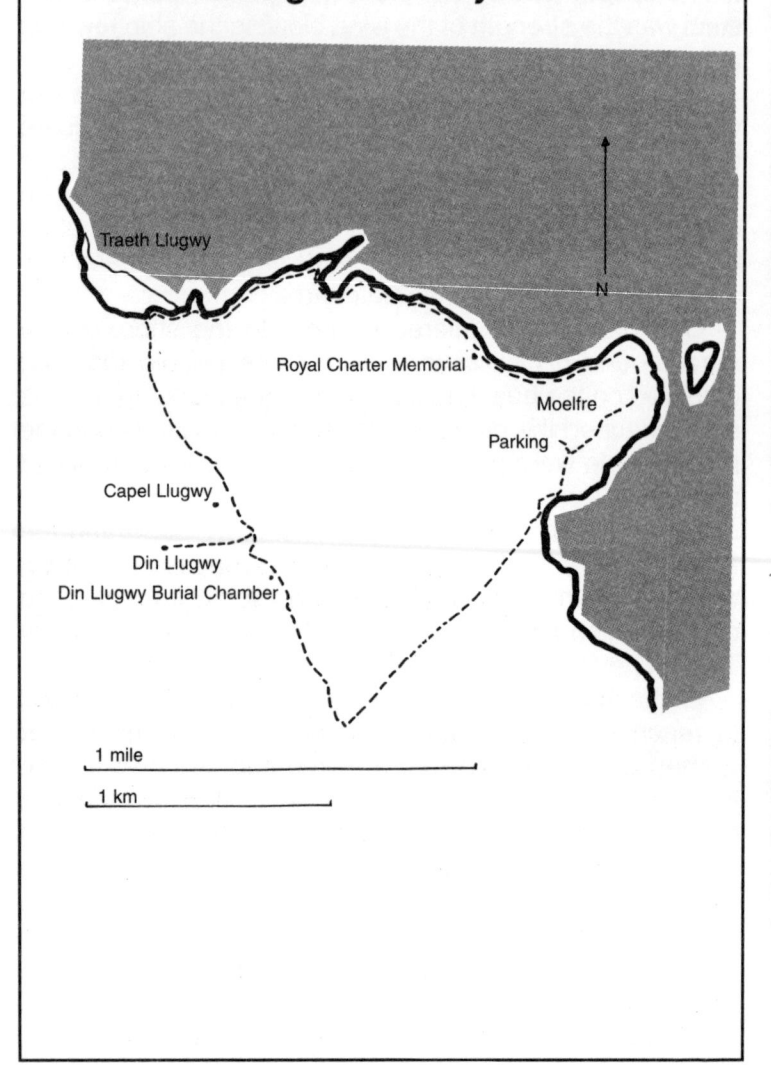

but the authorities failed to find the rest. There were stories in the area that the locals had found some of the gold and hidden it in their cottages. And sometime during the last century, whilst renovating a house in the area, a bag with gold pieces in it was found hidden in the chimney.

A memorial to those who lost their lives was raised on the top of the cliff that looks out over the sea where one of the worst disasters at sea in Britain happened.

THE WALK

From Moelfre past the remains of the ancient village of Din Llugwy to the beach at Traeth Llugwy, past the Royal Charter Memorial and back to Moelfre.
7 miles – 2½ hours

If you arrive by car, leave it in the car park on the way into Moelfre to the right of the bus stop, where you will also arrive if coming by bus.

Walk out of the car park, and turn in the direction of the bus stop and walk to the crossroads. Turn right and go up the hill to a roundabout. Follow the signs to Din Llugwy and Traeth Llugwy.

Walk carefully along the road and you will reach Din Llugwy Burial Chamber. Why not have a look around?

Then, return to the road, and continue along it until you see the sign to Din Llugwy on your left. This village dates back to before the Roman period and is worth visiting. On the way back you will see, to your left, an old church. This is Capel Llugwy; you can make a detour to visit it.

Go back to the road and turn left and walk in the same direction as you were before visiting Din Llugwy. At the crossroads, look carefully in both directions, and then go straight ahead, down the hill to the car park and beach at

Traeth Llugwy.

There is a shop in the car park during the summer selling drinks and ice cream. You now have a choice: you can either walk back to Moelfre along the cliff top path that starts by the shop or go down to the beach and walk to the left until you reach the end and then go up the steps to the top of the cliff.

Whatever your decision, you will then be walking along the cliff top path. Before you reach the caravan park on the right, you will see the Royal Charter memorial on a small hill with iron railings around it. Go past it until you see a stone stile; go over the stile and visit the memorial.

Then, go back to the cliff top path and walk through the caravan park. Follow the path until you come to open ground where it is difficult to find the path. Turn right, aiming for the houses. Then look for a pole with an arrow on it pointing up the field to a kissing gate.

Go through the gate and turn left, then through another gate and then go right past the cottages. Then turn left and go down hill towards Moelfre Lifeboat House. It is possible, at certain times, to visit the lifeboat house.

Then go to the left, past the Moelfre Seawatch Centre where you can find information on the area and the surrounding sea. Why not call in and have a look? Continue down to the beach at Moelfre. Near the small car park is a shop where they sell drinks and snacks.

After passing the shop you will see a large, black anchor. This is the anchor from another ship that sank in the area – the Hindlea. Then go up the hill to the crossroads, and turn left either to the bus stop or the car park where you started the walk.

DID YOU SEE THESE?

1. What animal is to be seen on the 'Welcome to Moelfre' sign?

   ....

2. When was the Llugwy Burial Chamber built?

   ....

3. According to the sign in Din Llugwy, what shape were the huts?

   ....

4. When was the south chapel of Capel Llugwy added?

   ....

5. According to the memorial, what type of ship was the Royal Charter?

   ....

6. What is the size of Moelfre's large lifeboat?

   ....

7. According to the sign near the Hindlea's anchor, when did she sink?

   ....

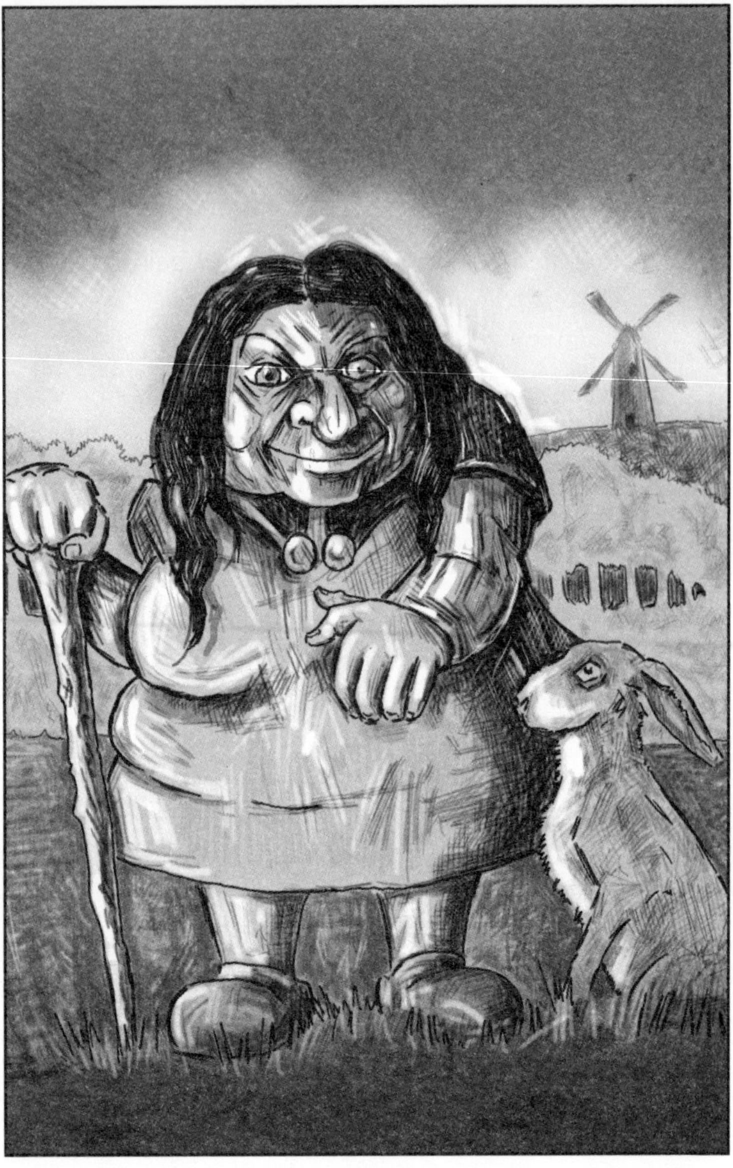

The Witches of Llanddona

THE STORY

One day, a boat full of men and women approached the beach at Llanddona. These people looked different to the people of Anglesey, they were smaller, their hair was pitch black and their skins were yellow. The people of Llanddona had seen them coming ashore and they rushed down to the beach to try and stop them, but they were too late. The strange visitors stood on the sand, wet and shivering. There were no sails, steering or oars on the boat, and it seems that they had been sent from somewhere for being witches. They has been at sea for a long time and they were hungry and thirsty.

The people of Llanddona stood in a circle around them, watching them. The strange people asked for water, but no one offered any. Suddenly, one of them struck the sand with a stick and a fountain of clear water appeared.

Everyone was frightened; who were these strange people who could do such tricks? They than let the strange people leave the beach and they walked up the hill towards Llanddona. When they arrived there, they started building rough houses of stones and branches. Once they had settled in, the men started smuggling goods to earn a living whilst the women would walk around the area begging for food and money. Everyone was afraid of them and no one refused to give them what they wanted.

When the witches went to the local market to buy a pig, no one would bid against them in case they were cursed.

Everyone in the village were afraid of them. Some said that they turned themselves into hares to make mischief. One day, a local man decided to try and get rid of one of them who had been a nuisance to him. He knew that an ordinary bullet would not kill a witch, therefore he put a piece of silver in his gun. He hit the witch and after that he had no trouble from him.

Another local man who was not afraid of them was Goronwy Tudur, but he had made every effort to keep them away from his house. Goronwy had grown a plant in front of his house which he knew the witches hated, and he had nailed a lucky horseshoe on every door that he had. He had also spread soil from the cemetery in every room, which was supposed to keep evil spirits away.

But one day he saw his cattle sitting in the field on their hind legs like cats. He knew that the witches had been there and had cursed the animals. Immediately, he burnt the skin of a snake and threw the ashes over the cows and they all, one by one, got up on four legs.

Another time, Goronwy was having difficulty making butter. He put the poker in the fire until it was red hot and then put it in the milk in the churn. Suddenly, a hare jumped out of the churn and ran away into the fields. It was one of the witches in disguise!

The most famous of the witches of Llanddona was Siân Bwt. Siân was very small, no more than about 110 centimetres high, so they say, and she had two thumbs on her left hand. Many say that the descendants of the

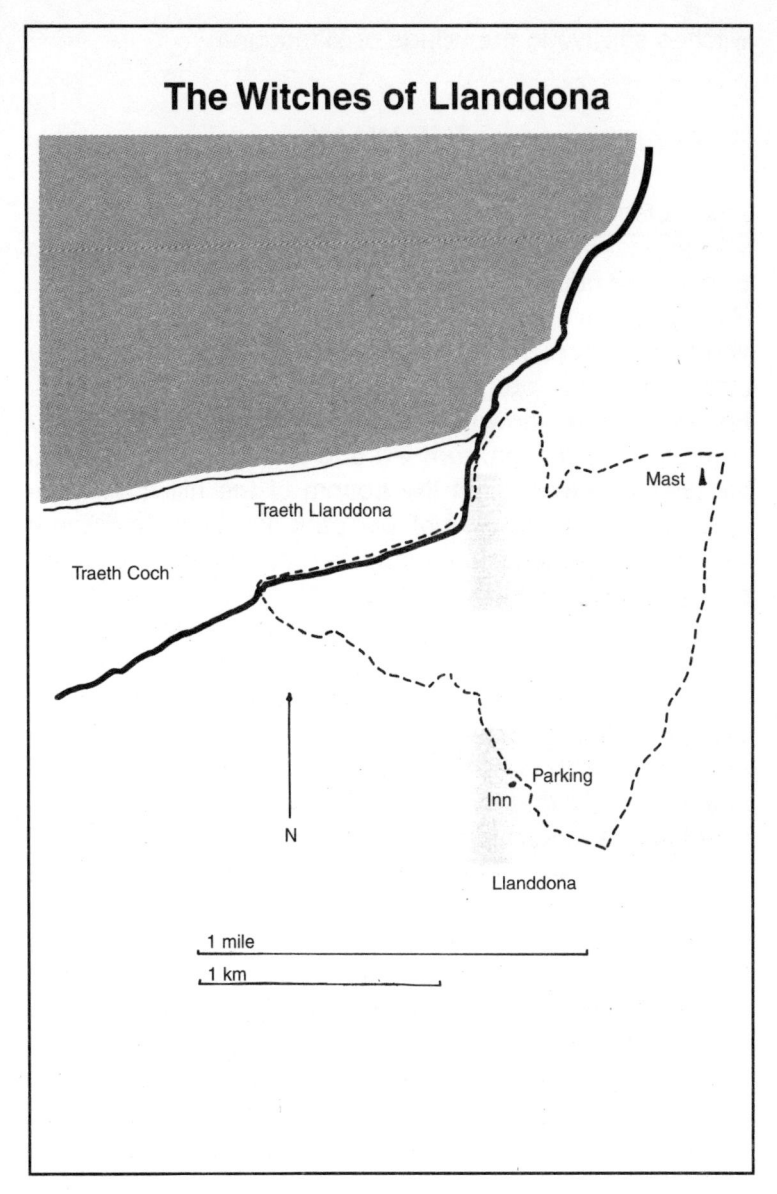

The Witches of Llanddona

witches still live in the village of Llanddona.

THE WALK

From Llanddona down to the beach and back into the village past the television mast.
6 miles – 2 hours

Park your car near the Owain Glyndŵr inn. For those of you coming by bus, there is a bus stop before reaching the inn. In front of you, you will see a sign 'To the Beach'. Follow the road down hill towards the beach. When you come to the junction, turn left and then go down a steep hill towards the sea. At the bottom of the hill, follow the road to the right to a small car park and Caban y Traeth where you can buy something to eat or drink on the beach during summer.

To your left you will see a path going through the dunes. Follow it and you will reach the sands of Traeth Llanddona. To your left is Traeth Coch or Red Wharf Bay. Here, centuries ago, there was a bitter battle between the Welsh and the Vikings who had just landed on Anglesey. So many were killed in the battle, that the beach was red with blood, and it was called traeth coch or red beach after that.

Turn right and walk along the beach to the far end where you will see a Coastal Path sign. Follow the path up the steps to a kissing gate. Go through the gate and along the side of the field, and then follow the path up the slope towards a bungalow. Go over the stile and through the gate near a cottage, and then up the road past some houses.

At the junction, turn left and go up the steep hill towards the television mast. From here you will have a magnificent view of Traeth Coch and Traeth Llanddona. Continue along the road to the mast and the junction. Turn right and walk along the right hand side of the road, facing the traffic. At the next junction, turn right and go back towards Llanddona. Go past the housing estate on the right and back to the Owain Glyndŵr inn.

DID YOU SEE THESE?

1. How many lions are there on Owain Glyndŵr's coat of arms?

   ....

2. What is the name of the house nearest the beach whilst going down the hill?

   ....

3. On the information sign in the car park near Llanddona beach, when are dogs prohibited from a part of the beach?

   ....

4. What is the name of the last house on the beach before you reach the path?

   ....

5. By the mast, what is the gradient of the hill?

   ....

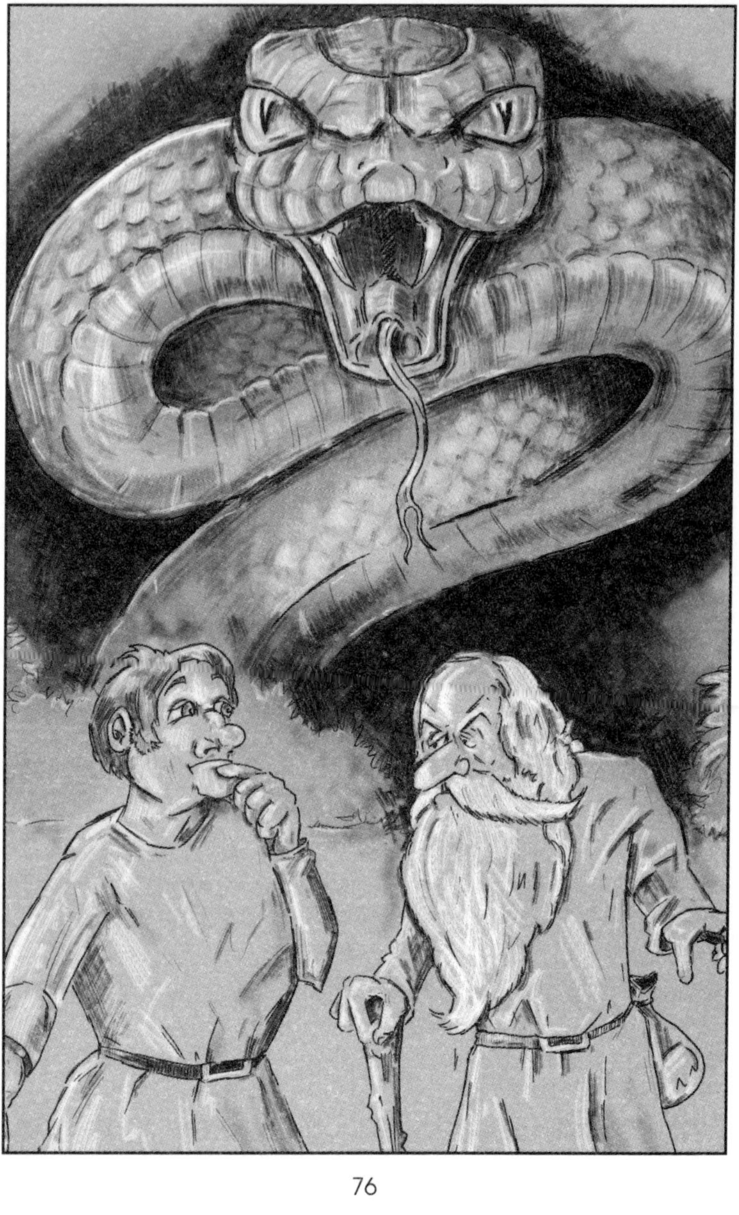

The Snake of Penhesgyn

THE STORY

One day, hundreds of years ago, an enormous snake came to live in the parish of Penmynydd. At the time, a man and his wife and their son lived in Penhesgyn farm. But one day, a wizard came to the house saying to the father that the snake, which lived on his land, would kill his son.

As he had only one son and as he had a lot of money, he arranged for his son to be sent to England to stay, far away from the enormous snake.

The snake hid in the brambles and gorse bushes and it was very difficult to catch it. Most of the people of Penmynydd were afraid of the snake. But there was one brave man in the area. One day he went to the snake's hideout, and whilst his friend kept a look out for the snake, he started digging a hole.

Then, he put a large, shiny pan over the hole. The following day, with the sun shining on the pan, the snake came out of its hole in the brambles and slid slowly towards the pan. There he saw another snake – exactly like itself! It did not realise that it was his reflection! It was not very happy that there was another giant snake living in the area, so he attacked it! Hissing and spitting its venom in every direction and swishing its long tail, it banged its head on the pan many times.

At last, there was no venom left in its fangs and it was

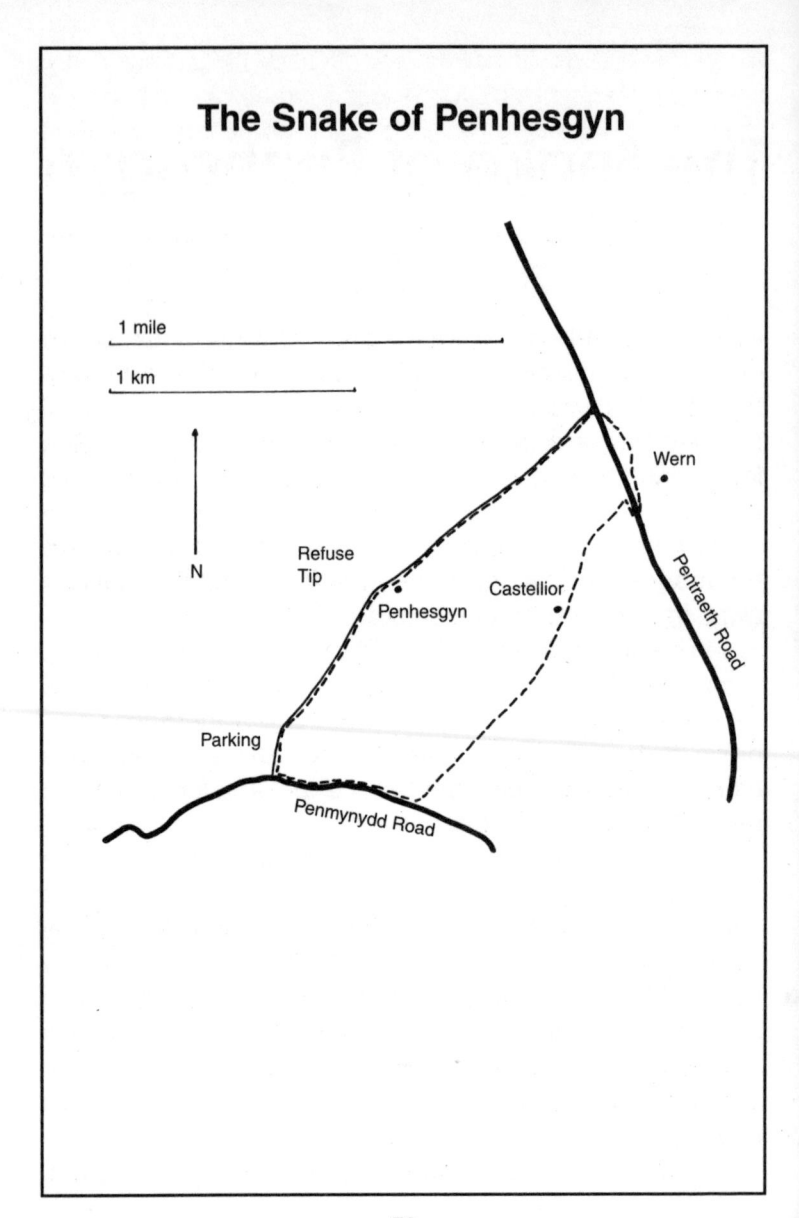

The Snake of Penhesgyn

so tired that it could not drag itself back to its hole in the brambles. The brave man was watching all this and he now crept out of his hiding place behind a gorse bush. He took out a heavy wooden club from his belt, and bashed the snake's head with it several times, killing it.

Everyone from the parish of Penmynydd came to see the huge, dead snake, and a message was sent to England to tell the son of Penhesgyn that the huge snake was dead and that it was safe for him to return home. All the men dug a huge hole and pushed the snake into it and covered it with soil.

The boy came home to Penhesgyn and the first thing that he wanted to do was to see the huge snake. The hole was opened and at the bottom was the skeleton of the snake. He went into the hole and kicked the snake's skeleton. "There you are," he said, kicking the snake's skull, "for causing so much trouble for everyone!"

But, as the boy came from a rich family, his shoes were made of thin, expensive leather, not like the heavy shoes the other people wore. Because of this, one of the snake's fangs went through his shoe and into his foot. There was still a tiny drop of venom in the fang – enough to kill the son, and he fell to the ground, as dead as the snake.

The words of the wizard had come true!

THE WALK

From the Penmynydd road past Penhesgyn to the Pentraeth road and back past Castellior.
3½ miles – 1½ hours
From the Penmynydd road (which runs between Menai Bridge and Llangefni), look for the Refuse Tip sign. Go in

the direction of the tip, and then after a few metres you will find a place to park the car by Penhesgyn Newydd. Buses travel along the Penmynydd road and you can ask the driver to put you down by the Refuse Tip sign.

Walk along the road, past Penhesgyn Hall and the entrance to the refuse tip. Be careful on this road, as there are lorries constantly travelling to the tip. It might be a good idea if you made this journey over the weekend when there is less traffic.

Continue along the road, with magnificent views of the Snowdonia range on your left. Go past Penhesgyn farm on the right and after a while you will reach the main road which runs from Menai Bridge to Benllech – the Pentraeth road. Turn right and walk along the grass verge until you are opposite a bus stop. Cross the road here – carefully, as it is a busy road.

After crossing the road, go straight ahead and follow the old road past Wern farm until you come back to the main road. Cross the road carefully once again, and then walk to the right along the pavement to the entrance to Castellior farm. Go down the lane towards the farm, and follow the lane to the left through the farm yard past an impressive building and then past Castellior farmhouse.

Continue along the lane until you come to a cattle grid. Go over it and then turn right and walk along the road until you come to the main road – the Penmynydd road.

Walk carefully on the right hand side of the road, on the grass verge when possible. Go past Hen Efail (the old smithy) and Hen Dyrpeg (the old turnpike) on the right until you reach the Refuse Tip sign. Either catch a bus or go right back to the car.

DID YOU SEE THESE?

1. What are the licence numbers of the refuse tip?

   ....

2. What is the name of the bungalow on the left before reaching the Pentraeth road?

   ....

3. On the sign on the Pentraeth road, how many miles to Llanfairpwll?

   ....

4. How many Tourist Board stars has Wern farm?

   ....

5. Near the Castellior farm sign, there is the name of another house. What is it?

   ....

6. What is the name of the house nearest the refuse tip sign?

   ....

These are the birds that I saw	These are the animals that I saw	These are the flowers that I saw

These are the birds that I saw	These are the animals that I saw	These are the flowers that I saw

These are the birds that I saw	These are the animals that I saw	These are the flowers that I saw